Martin Luther King, Jr., was one of th[e]
leaders. A preacher and practical phil[osopher]
message into the streets, where his w[ords]
instruments of profound social change. In this uniquely
accessible A-to-Z collection, Dr. King and his legacy of
eloquent wisdom, gathered from books, letters, speeches,
sermons, and other sources, are brought to life. Here are
some samples of his ideas and ideals:

LOVE: Power without love is reckless and abusive and ...
love without power is sentimental and anemic. Power at
its best is love implementing the demands of justice.

CRIMINALS: The most dangerous criminal may be the
man gifted with reason, but with no morals.

MONEY: Money, like any other force such as electricity, is
amoral and can be used for either good or evil.

REVENGE: In spite of the fact that the law of revenge
solves no social problems, men continue to follow its
disastrous leading. History is cluttered with the
wreckage of nations and individuals that pursued this
self-defeating path.

The Wisdom of
MARTIN LUTHER KING, JR.

ALEX AYRES is the editor of *The Wit* [and Wisdom of] *Mark
Twain* and *The Wit and Wisdom of A*[braham Lincoln,] b[oth]
available in Meridian editions. He [...]
Running Times and the *Harvard* [...]
have appeared in *Forbes*.

Also edited by Alex Ayres

The Wit and Wisdom of Abraham Lincoln
The Wit and Wisdom of Mark Twain

The Wisdom of

MARTIN LUTHER KING, Jr.

EDITED BY
ALEX AYRES

A MERIDIAN BOOK

MERIDIAN
Published by the Penguin Group
Penguin Books USA Inc., 375 Hudson Street,
New York, New York 10014, U.S.A.
Penguin Books Ltd, 27 Wrights Lane, London W8 5TZ, England
Penguin Books Australia Ltd, Ringwood, Victoria, Australia
Penguin Books Canada Ltd, 10 Alcorn Avenue,
Toronto, Ontario, Canada M4V 3B2
Penguin Books (N.Z.) Ltd, 182-190 Wairau Road,
Auckland 10, New Zealand

Penguin Books Ltd, Registered Offices:
Harmondsworth, Middlesex, England

First published by Meridian, an imprint of New American
Library, a division of Penguin Books USA Inc.

First Printing, January, 1993
10 9 8 7 6 5 4 3 2 1

Copyright © Alex Ayres, 1993
All rights reserved

REGISTERED TRADEMARK—MARCA REGISTRADA

Library of Congress Cataloging-in-Publication Data

The Wisdom of Martin Luther King, Jr. / edited by Alex Ayres.
   p.   cm.
  ISBN 0-452-01104-3
  I. King, Martin Luther, Jr., 1929–1968—Philosophy. 2. King,
Martin Luther, Jr., 1929–1968—Quotations. I. Ayres, Alex.
E185.97.K5A25 1993
323′.092—dc20   92–18999
                                  CIP

Printed in the United States of America
Set in Palatino

to the Spirit of Synthesis

ACKNOWLEDGMENTS

Thanks to Dr. King for his inspiration and guidance, then and now.

Thanks to all those whose names are not mentioned here, but without whose courage and goodness the Freedom Movement could have claimed no victories.

Thanks to Coretta Scott King, the King family and trustees, Ralph Abernathy, and those who knew Martin best, for sharing their memories and insights.

Thanks to HarperCollins and the Joan Daves Agency for their permissions. Thanks to Arnold Dolin, Hugh Rawson, Julia Moskin, and Paula Smith for their help with the manuscript. Thanks to John Ayres, Alice Ayres, Pam Ayres, and my family for their support.

Thanks to the authors, scholars, teachers, preachers, activists, and practitioners of nonviolent resistance who keep Dr. King's legacy alive.

Thanks to you for keeping Dr. King's dream alive.

MARTIN LUTHER KING, JR.

Have we, in America, had a hero in our time—that is, since World War II? I can only think of one man with a serious claim, Martin Luther King. The theme was high, the occasion noble, the stage open to the world's eye, the courage clear and against odds. And martyrdom came to purge all dross away. King seems to be made for the folk consciousness, and the folk consciousness is the Valhalla of the true hero—not the gossip column.

—Robert Penn Warren,
"A Dearth of Heroes," 1972

I see an America in which Martin Luther King's dream is our national dream.

—Jimmy Carter

Martin Luther King is the most notorious liar in the country.

—J. Edgar Hoover,
FBI director

Martin Luther King spoke with the tongues of men and of angels.

—Dr. L. Harold DeWolf,
Teacher of King

I don't think America has yet learned to appreciate the greatness of Martin Luther King, Jr.

—Reverend Fred Shuttlesworth,
Civil rights leader

In him the word became flesh and dwelt among men.

—Reverend Jesse Jackson,
Civil rights leader

I think his important legacy is that human problems, no matter how big, can be solved ... and organizing to solve those problems is an ongoing process.

—Reverend Andrew Young,
U.N. ambassador, civil rights leader

Martin Luther King represents a voice, a vision, and a way. And I invite all of you to take seriously this voice, this vision, and this way.... I am convinced that the whole future of America depends on how seriously we take this voice, this vision, and this way.

—Rabbi Abraham Heschel,
Introducing King to Jewish leaders, March 1968

People loved King.... I've seen people in the South climb over each other just to say, "I touched him! I touched him!" ... I'm even talking about the young. The old people had more love and respect. They even saw him like a god.

—Stokely Carmichael,
Black Power advocate

Martin Luther King died as he lived, fighting to his last breath for justice. In only twelve years of public life he evoked more respect for black people than a preceding century had produced. We who knew him intimately cannot recall a single instance when he expressed a word of hatred for any man. Yet his indictment of segregation, discrimination, and poverty was a hurricane of fire that opened a new era of struggle for freedom.

—Harry Belafonte and Stanley Levison, joint statement after King's assassination

King used the biblical symbols that are at the heart of American civil religion and gave them fresh meaning.

—John Dixon Elder,
Clergyman and author

We thank you for telling us, in the life and death of Martin Luther King, Jr., that peace and justice are possible. History is not fate. We shall not be humiliated and suffer forever.... We have King as our tomorrow.

—Shun P. Govender,
South African anti-apartheid activist

For me and for many of his youthful critics, King became wiser as we grew older.... If King were alive today, he would doubtless encourage those who celebrate his life to recognize their responsibility to struggle as he did for a more just and peaceful world.... He would probably be the unpopular social critic he was on the eve of the Poor People's campaign rather than the object of national homage that he became after his death. His basic message would be the same as it was when he was alive, for he did not bend with the changing political winds.

—Clayborne Carson,
Clergyman and author

He was a genius. I am not talking about my son when I say that, I'm talking about a world citizen. He moved beyond us early. He did not belong to us, he belonged to the world.

—Reverend Martin Luther King, Sr.

As a proponent of nonviolent resistance, he holds out the only slim hope for social sanity in a violence-ridden world; as an American prophet, he commands the respect even of those who opposed him; and as an egalitarian internationalist, he inspires all oppressed peoples around the world who struggle for democracy, freedom, and equality.

—Cornell West,
Clergyman and author

Martin Luther King, Jr., was the conscience of his generation. A Southerner, a black man, he gazed upon the great wall of segregation and saw that the power of love could bring it down.

From pain and exhaustion of his fight to free all people from the bondage of separation and injustice, he wrung his eloquent statement of his dream of what America could be.

He helped us overcome our ignorance of one another. He spoke out against a war he felt was unjust as he had spoken out against laws that were unfair.

He made our nation stronger because he made it better. Honored by kings, he continued to his last days to strive for a world where the poorest and humblest among us could enjoy the fulfillment of the promises of our founding fathers.

His life informed us, his dreams sustain us yet.

—Citation, posthumous award of the Presidential Medal of Freedom,
July 4, 1977

WHY READ THIS BOOK?

A single bullet in Memphis, Tennessee, brought an end to the life of one of history's greatest champions of freedom. No one can replace Martin Luther King, Jr. Nor is it necessary or desirable that he be replaced. His wisdom, his ideas, his ideals, his eloquence, and his spiritual leadership are all still available to us today.

We do not do justice to the greatness of the man if we honor his memory but forget his message. If we don't know what his message was, we don't know what he stood for, what he lived for, and what he died for.

Martin Luther King showed us what one individual can do to transform the world for the better. Such is the legacy of his life. But he also left us the legacy of his words, his works, and the wisdom he bequeathed to us through them.

King was one of America's greatest philosophers, but he wasn't the type of philosopher who sits quietly in tranquil solitude, contemplating truth and beauty. He was a practical philosopher in the American tradition of Jefferson, Franklin, and Lincoln. He was a man of ideas who put those ideas into practice and transformed the world. He was a thinking man who successfully applied philosophical principles toward solving humanity's most difficult problems in the turmoil and tumult of the real world in crisis.

King was a genius of synthesis, combining and reconciling contraries to create a greater and more harmonious whole. Although he is known for desegregation, it is *integration* that he championed: the synthesis of separate black and white societies. Although he is known for the principle of nonviolence, it is *nonviolent resistance* that he championed: the synthesis of nonviolence and strong resistance against injustice.

Dr. King is not just a spokesman for African-Americans. He is a spokesman for the conscience of America as it strives to realize its original dream of freedom and equality. He is a spokesman for humanity as the human race strives to realize its universal dream of peace and brotherhood.

In the final analysis King is, like Christ and Gandhi before him, a philosopher of love. He is a spokesman for love that is justice in action—nonviolent in nature—and that is liberation in progress.

If we no longer hear the voice of Martin Luther King, it is probably because we are not listening. But if we ignore him, it is at the risk of our own humanity.

The Wisdom of Martin Luther King, Jr., is for the reader who would like to know what Dr. King said on a variety of subjects—and what he is still saying to us today.

A

ABERNATHY, RALPH

Martin Luther King and his friend Reverend Ralph Abernathy were preparing to leave their room at the Lorraine Motel in Memphis to go to dinner.

"Let me put on my cologne," said Abernathy, stepping into the bathroom.

"I'll wait on the balcony." King hesitated. "Ralph?"

"Yes?"

"Ralph, don't ever employ anybody on staff of SCLC that uses violence to reach our goals, even on a temporary basis."

It was a strange thing for King to say. As President of the Southern Christian Leadership Conference, King was in charge of all hiring decisions. Abernathy reflected on this moment later: "And I wondered, why is he telling me this? But I concluded that he was telling me only because I was the treasurer of the organization."

Abernathy was so puzzled by this remark he didn't know what to say. He had sprinkled Aramis on his hands, and as he was raising his hands to pat his face he was startled by a loud sound. At first he thought it was a firecracker.

Emerging from the bathroom, Abernathy saw King sprawled on his back on the balcony. He had been shot through the neck from a telescopic rifle across the street.

Martin Luther King, only thirty-nine years old, was dead.

Ralph Abernathy was King's successor as President of the Southern Christian Leadership Conference. He never forgot Dr. King's last request.

(see ASSASSINATION)

ACHIEVEMENT

"After one has discovered what he is made for, he should surrender all of the power in his being to the achievement of this. He should seek to do it so well that nobody could do it better."

Martin Luther King offered this advice in his favorite sermon, "Three Dimensions of a Complete Life." It was the sermon he delivered in Boston the day his fiancée Coretta Scott first saw him preach in 1952. It was the sermon he preached in his trial sermon at Dexter Avenue Baptist Church in Montgomery, Alabama, to win his first pulpit in 1954. It was the sermon he preached in St. Paul's Cathedral in London on his way to Oslo to receive the Nobel Peace Prize in 1964.

In this sermon King urged excellence in work, no matter what that work might be. "No work is insignificant," he declared. "If a man is called a street sweeper, he should sweep streets even as Michelangelo painted, or Beethoven composed music, or Shakespeare wrote poetry. He should sweep streets so well that all the host of heaven and earth will pause to say, 'Here lived a great street sweeper who did his job well.'"

2

Martin Luther King was in Memphis in support of striking sanitation workers when he was assassinated on April 4, 1968.

(see EXCELLENCE)

ACTIVISM

"Freedom is *never* given to *anybody!*" bellowed 26-year-old Martin Luther King to a packed church on the first day of the Montgomery Bus Boycott, December 5, 1956. "For the oppressor has you in domination because he plans to *keep* you there! And he never voluntarily gives it up."

Activism is necessary to achieve liberation, according to King, because oppression does not yield unless strong pressure is applied against it by the oppressed.

"We've got to keep on keepin' on in order to gain freedom," he told the assembly in Montgomery. "It is not done voluntarily. It is done through the pressure that comes about from people who are oppressed. Privileged classes never give up their privileges without strong resistance."

Where Dr. King differed from many other social activists was in his insistence that the most effective form of activism is nonviolent direct action.

(see NONVIOLENCE, DIRECT ACTION, PRESSURE)

ACTIVIST

The conscience of an awakened activist cannot be satisfied with a focus on local problems, if only because he sees that local problems are all interconnected with world problems.

—*The Trumpet of Conscience*, pp. 49–50

ADVICE

In his sermon "Three Dimensions of a Complete Life," King tells the story of a "wise old preacher" who offers advice to a young man named Robert.

The preacher delivered the commencement address on the day Robert graduated from college.

After the speech, Robert came up to the preacher to shake his hand. The preacher asked Robert his plans for the future.

Robert said he planned to go to law school, expecting the preacher to be impressed.

"What then?" asked the preacher.

Robert said he planned to establish a law practice, expecting the preacher to be impressed.

"What then?" asked the preacher.

Robert said he planned to make a lot of money, retire early, and travel around the world, which is what he always wanted to do.

"What then?" asked the preacher.

Robert shrugged. "Those are all my plans."

The preacher shook his head. "Young man, your plans are far too small. They can extend only seventy-five or a hundred years at the most. You must make your plans big enough to include God and large enough to include eternity."

(see GOD, GREATNESS, SERVICE)

AFFLUENCE

All too many of those who live in affluent America ignore those who exist in poor America; in doing so, the affluent Americans will eventually have to face themselves with the question that Eichmann chose to ignore: How responsible am I for the well-being of my fellows?

—*Where Do We Go from Here: Chaos or Community?* pp. 85–86

4

AFRAID

"Don't be afraid!" King exhorted an audience in Birmingham in the spring of 1963.

"When I say don't be afraid, you know what I really mean. Don't even be afraid to die. For I submit to you tonight, no man is free if he fears death."

On the last day of his life, a few hours before his assassination, when King was meeting with his staff at the Lorraine Motel in Memphis, several colleagues voiced concern about reported threats of assassination.

King shook his head and said, "I'd rather be dead than afraid."

(see DEATH)

AFRO-AMERICANS

The Negro is the child of two cultures—Africa and America . . . all too many Negroes seek to embrace only one side of their natures. . . . The American Negro is neither totally African nor totally western. He is Afro-American, a true hybrid, a combination of two cultures.

—*Where Do We Go from Here?* p. 53
(see SYNTHESIS)

AFTERLIFE

When Coretta Scott first dated Martin Luther King, the conversation eventually turned to religion. Coretta was surprised by his response when she asked him about the afterlife.

"I'm much more concerned about this life than the life after," he said with a shrug. "I'm not concerned with the temperature of hell or the furnishings of heaven, but with the things men do here on earth."

(see DEATH, HEAVEN, KINGDOM OF GOD)

AGE

There was something strange about Martin Luther King's age. It seemed to vary depending on the circumstances and the observer.

He often struck people as older than his years. When Coretta Scott first met him, her initial impression was of an "older man," although he was actually younger than she was. As a leader and a public speaker, he exhibited a maturity that belied his youth. His prodigious achievements led to his becoming the youngest Nobel Peace Prize winner in history at the age of 35.

But there was another side to him that the public did not see: a young and playful side. It was part of his personality to the very end of his life. On the afternoon of his assassination he engaged in a pillow fight with Andrew Young.

Coretta Scott's mother noticed this playful quality in Martin Luther King when she saw him in Boston in the summer of 1954. On Sunday morning she watched him preach an impressive sermon. That afternoon she accompanied him and Coretta to an amusement park, where Martin insisted on going on all of the hair-raising rides and spent the balance of the afternoon roller-skating, doing fancy turns and faltering flips, falling down and clowning around.

Mrs. Scott could hardly believe it was the same serious-minded man who had delivered such a wise and uplifting sermon a few hours earlier. "You know," she chuckled, "you act like you are about four years old."

"You're as old as you act," King replied, roller-skates in hand. "Why should I get to be four years old only once?"

(see HUMOR)

AGITATION

The Negro has not gained a single right in America without persistent pressure and agitation.

—Where Do We Go from Here? p. 90

ALBANY, GEORGIA

One of the most frustrating episodes in King's civil rights career was the Albany, Georgia, campaign in 1962, where a planned March to the Sea was stymied by a federal court injunction. After a marathon week of meetings, legal battles, and confrontations with segregationists, King received the consolation of a visit from Coretta for the weekend.

The Albany campaign did not end in success, but in later years Martin would joke: "I thank the Lord for the stamina that allowed me to accomplish something positive in Albany that weekend. That was when my fourth child, Bernice, was conceived."

(see Biography 1962, INJUNCTIONS)

ALIENATION

Alienation, warned King in a 1967 lecture titled "Youth and Social Action," is one of the most dangerous evils in the world today.

Alienation is an evil force because it separates and divides. All of the forces of good in the world are founded in interconnectedness and unity—of man and man, man and woman, man and nature, man and God.

"Growth requires connection and trust. Alienation is a form of living death. It is the acid of despair that dissolves society."

* * *

Gargantuan industry and government, woven into an intricate computerized mechanism, leave the person outside. The sense of participation is lost, the feeling that ordinary individuals influence important decisions vanishes, and man becomes separated and diminished.

When an individual is no longer a true participant, when he no longer feels a sense of responsibility to his society, the content of democracy is emptied.

When culture is degraded and vulgarity enthroned, when the social system does not build security but induces peril, inexorably the individual is impelled to pull away from a soulless society.

This produces alienation—perhaps the most pervasive and insidious development in contemporary society.

—*The Trumpet of Conscience*, p. 44

"ALL HERE AND NOW ..."

King adopted a four-word slogan—All Here and Now!—which he sometimes used to rally the crowd at civil rights assemblies. He tried it out in a successful speech at an NAACP meeting on July 5, 1962.

"All. Here. And now!" he called out while the crowd applauded rhythmically. "We want *all* of our rights. We want our freedom *here* in America. Here behind the cotton curtain of Alabama. Here on the red clay of Georgia.

"And *now*. We have lived with gradualism, and we know that it is nothing but do-nothingism and escapism which ends up in stand-stillism.

"We want freedom *now*!

"All here and now!"

(see FREEDOM NOW, MARCHING RHETORIC)

ALTRUISM

True altruism is more than the capacity to pity; it is the capacity to sympathize. Pity may represent little more than the impersonal concern which prompts the mailing of a check, but true sympathy is the personal concern which demands the giving of one's soul.

—*The Strength to Love*, p. 21

AMERICA

The goal of America is freedom.

—Letter from Birmingham Jail, 1963

We chose as our motto: "To save the soul of America."

—*The Trumpet of Conscience*, p. 24

Ever since the signing of the Declaration of Independence, America has manifested a schizophrenic personality on the question of race. She has been torn between selves—a self in which she has proudly professed democracy and a self in which she has sadly practiced the antithesis of democracy.

—*Stride Toward Freedom*, p. 190

We feel that we are the conscience of America. We are its troubled soul. We will continue to insist that right be done because both God's Will and the heritage of our nation speak through our echoing demands.

—Speech, August 5, 1962
Statement from jail in Albany, Georgia

If America would come to herself and return to her true home, "one nation, indivisible, with liberty and justice for all," she would give the democratic creed a new authentic ring, enkindle the imagination of mankind and fire the souls of men.

—*Where Do We Go from Here?* p. 84

America, I don't plan to let you rest until that day comes into being when all God's children will be respected. . . . America, I don't plan to allow you to rest until from every city hall in this country, justice will roll down like waters and righteousness like a mighty stream. . . .

America, I don't plan to let you rest until you live it out that "all . . . are created equal and endowed by their creator with certain inalienable rights."

—Sermon, "Which Way Its Soul Shall Go," August 2, 1967

We must begin to ask, "Why are there forty million poor people in a nation overflowing with unbelievable affluence?" Why has our nation placed itself in the position of being God's military agent on earth . . . ? Why have we substituted the arrogant undertaking of policing the whole world for the high task of putting our own house in order?

—*Where Do We Go from Here?* p. 133

Your moral progress lags behind your scientific progress, your mentality outdistances your morality, and your civilization outshines your culture. . . . Through your scientific genius you have made of the world a neighborhood, but you have failed to employ your moral and spiritual genius to make of it a neighborhood.

—*The Strength to Love*, p. 129

The thing wrong with America is white racism.

—Speech, Laurel, Mississippi, March 19, 1968

If America is to remain a first-class nation, it cannot have a second-class citizenship.

—*Stride Toward Freedom*, p. 197

In our own American struggle for freedom and justice, we are seeing the death of evil.

—*The Strength to Love*, p. 61
(see also FREEDOM)

AMERICAN DEMOCRACY

The great glory of American democracy is the right to protest for right.

—Speech, Montgomery, Alabama, December 5, 1955

The future of America is bound up with the solution of the present crisis. The shape of the world today does not permit us the luxury of a faltering democracy.

—*Stride Toward Freedom*, p. 197
(see DEMOCRACY, NOW)

AMERICAN DREAM

In a commencement address at Pennsylvania's Lincoln University, King expressed his view that "America is essentially a dream." The Civil Rights movement, he said, was a collective effort to reduce the gap between the nation's ideals and its practices, and to restore America to its original dream.

In his letter from Birmingham City Jail he wrote that those who participated in sit-ins to protest segregation in Birmingham were affirming the American Dream.

"One day the South will know that when these disinherited children of God sat down at lunch counters, they were in reality standing up for what is best in the American dream and for the most sacred values in our Judeo-

11

Christian heritage, thereby bringing our nation back to those great wells of democracy which were dug deep by the founding fathers in their formulation of the Constitution and the Declaration of Independence."

It is a dream of a land where men of all races, of all nationalities, and of all creeds can live together as brothers. The substance of the dream is expressed in these sublime words, words lifted to cosmic proportions: "We hold these truths to be self-evident; that all men are created equal; that they are endowed by their Creator with certain inalienable rights; that among these are life, liberty, and the pursuit of happiness." This is the dream.

—*Negro History Bulletin*, vol. 31, no. 5, May 1968, p. 10
(see also DREAM)

AMERICAN REVOLUTION

The first man to die in the American Revolution was a Negro seaman, Crispus Attucks. Before that fateful struggle ended, the institution of absolute monarchy was laid on its deathbed. We may now be in only the initial period of an era of change as far-reaching in its consequences as the American Revolution.

—*The Trumpet of Conscience*, p. 17
(see also WORLD REVOLUTION)

AMERICANS

The majority of white Americans consider themselves sincerely committed to justice for the Negro. They believe that American society is essentially hospitable to fair play and to steady growth toward a middle-class Utopia embodying racial harmony. But unfortunately this is a fantasy of self-deception and comfortable vanity. Overwhelmingly America is still struggling with irresolution and contradictions. It has been sincere and even ardent in welcoming some change. But too quickly apathy and disinterest rise to the surface when the next logical steps are to be taken.

—*Where Do We Go from Here?* pp. 4–5

If Americans permit thought-control, business-control, and freedom-control to continue, we shall surely move within the shadows of fascism.

—*The Strength to Love*, p. 11

If an American is concerned only about his nation, he will not be concerned about the peoples of Asia, Africa, or South America. Is this not why nations engage in the madness of war without the slightest sense of penitence? Is this not why the murder of a citizen of your own nation is a crime, but the murder of citizens of another nation in war is an act of heroic virtue?

—*The Strength to Love*, p. 18
(see INTERDEPENDENCE, MODERATES, WORLD PERSPECTIVE)

ANGER

"You must not harbor anger," I admonished myself. "You must be willing to suffer the anger of the opponent, and yet not return anger. You must not become bitter. No matter how emotional your opponents are, you must become calm."

—Advice to himself in *Stride Toward Freedom*, p. 121
(see BITTERNESS, HATRED, NONVIOLENCE)

APATHY

It is still one of the tragedies of human history that the "children of darkness" are frequently more determined and zealous than the "children of light."

—*Stride Toward Freedom*, p. 119

History will have to record that the greatest tragedy of this period of social transition was not the strident clamor of the bad people, but the appalling silence of the good people.

—*Stride Toward Freedom*, p. 202

Apathy among the Negroes themselves is also a factor. Even where the polls are open to all, Negroes have shown themselves too slow to exercise their voting privileges.

—*Stride Toward Freedom*, p. 222

In the past, apathy was a moral failure. Today, it is a form of moral and political suicide.

—*Stride Toward Freedom*, p. 222
(see EVIL, VOTE)

APOCALYPSE

The apocalypse preached by Martin Luther King was one in which all human polarities—white and black, rich and poor, male and female, spirit and flesh—come together. "I can hear Isaiah again," he told his congregation in April 1957, "because it has a profound meaning to me. That somehow 'every valley shall be exalted, every hill shall be made low, the crooked places shall be made straight, and the rough places plains. The glory of the Lord shall be revealed, and all flesh shall see it together.' And that's the beauty of this thing. *All* flesh shall see it together. . . .

"Not some white and some black, not some yellow and some brown, but all flesh shall see it together. They shall see it from Montgomery! They shall see it from New York! They shall see it from Ghana! They shall see it from China!

"For I can look out and see a great number, as John saw, marching into the great eternity, because God is working in this world and at this hour and at this moment. And God grants that we will get on board and start marching with God, because we got orders now to break down the bondage and the walls of colonialism, exploitation, and imperialism, to break them down to the point that no man will trample over another man, but that all men will respect the dignity and worth of all human personality.

"And then we will be in Canaan's freedom land. Moses might not get to see Canaan, but his children will see it. He even got to the mountaintop enough to see it, and that assured him that it was coming."

(see Biography 1968, SYNTHESIS)

ARMS RACE

The nations have believed that greater armaments will cast out fear. But alas! They have produced greater fear.

—*The Strength to Love*, p. 112

Somehow we must transform the dynamics of the world power struggle from the nuclear arms race, which no one can win, to a creative contest to harness man's genius for the purpose of making peace and prosperity a reality for all the nations of the world. In short, we must shift the arms race into a "peace race."

—*Where Do We Go from Here?* p. 185
(see DISARMAMENT, PEACE, WAR)

ARTIFICIAL FLOWERS

On March 12, 1968, three weeks before his assassination, Martin Luther King sent a bouquet of artificial flowers—red carnations—to his wife Coretta in Atlanta. He called her on the phone. "Did you get your flowers?" he asked.

She thanked him for the flowers, but asked him why he had chosen synthetic ones. "You never gave me artificial flowers before," she said, pleased and puzzled at the same time.

Martin replied, "I wanted to give you something you could always keep."

It was as if he somehow knew he would never again be able to send his wife flowers, so he wanted these flowers to last.

ASSASSINATION

King journeyed to Memphis, Tennessee, to support a sanitation workers' strike on March 28, 1968. He came to participate in what was supposed to be a nonviolent protest march. He considered it a "prelude" to the Poor People's Campaign he was planning to take to Washington in April.

Twelve thousand protesters marched down Beale Street. Only five minutes after King joined the march, it turned into a nightmare. Someone smashed a window in Pape's Men's Shop, and the sound of the breaking glass seemed to set off a chain reaction. Police stormed into the crowd with billy clubs and tear gas canisters. A sixteen-year-old black, identified by the police as a looter, was shot and killed. There were sixty other injuries and more than two hundred arrests.

It was the nadir of King's career. Never before had a demonstration in which he participated turned violent. He was deeply depressed. He resolved to return to Memphis again and schedule a new march to demonstrate that nonviolence was not dead.

He returned to Memphis on Wednesday, April 3. That night he spoke at the Masonic Temple to a crowd of two thousand people. It was his last public address. It concluded with words that were eerily prophetic.

"Well, I don't know what will happen now. We've got some difficult days ahead. But it really doesn't matter with me now, because I've been to the mountaintop. And I don't mind. Like anybody, I would like to live a long life.

Longevity has its place. But I'm not concerned about that now. I just want to do God's will. And He's allowed me to go up to the mountain, and I've looked over, and I've seen the promised land. I may not get there with you. But I want you to know tonight that we, as a people, will get to the promised land. And so I'm happy tonight. I'm not worried about anything. I'm not fearing any man. Mine eyes have seen the glory of the coming of the Lord."

The next day, Thursday, he met with some of his aides in Room 306, a second-story room he was sharing with Ralph Abernathy at the Lorraine Motel. His mood was variable. When Andrew Young came back from the federal court, where he'd been arguing for Monday's parade permit, King appeared distraught at first, but then a playful spirit came over him, and they wound up having a pillow fight.

At six in the evening King had just finished dressing for dinner. While waiting for Abernathy, who was still in the bathroom, King stepped out onto the balcony. He exchanged a few words with some friends who were in the parking lot below waiting for him. He waved and turned to go inside to get his coat. Suddenly a single shot rang out. The fatal bullet struck King in the neck.

The rifle was fired from the bathroom window of the boardinghouse across the street at 422½ South Main, two hundred yards away, where a tall, thin white man signing his name as "John Willard" had registered that afternoon at 3:15. Paying for a week in advance, he had insisted on a back room. An hour later this individual had purchased a pair of Bushnell binoculars and taken them to his room, along with a Remington 30.06 telescopic rifle and a box of soft-point bullets.

After firing the single fatal shot through the window of the bathroom, which was adjacent to his rented room, the assassin wrapped the rifle in a sheet and dropped it on the sidewalk before escaping in a getaway car, a white Mustang later found abandoned in Atlanta.

Two months later, on June 8, after an international manhunt, a 40-year-old escaped convict named James Earl Ray was arrested at Heathrow Airport in London. The fugitive's movements had been traced by the FBI from Memphis to Toronto, where he arrived on April 8, and finally to London, where he flew on May 6.

Ray claimed he was innocent. He said he had been employed, instructed, and "set up" by a red-haired French Canadian man named Raoul. Ray hired the prominent attorney Percy Foreman, famous for defending accused murderers. Two weeks before the trial, Foreman persuaded Ray to sign an agreement to plead guilty in exchange for a ninety-nine-year sentence. No defense arguments were presented at the trial on March 10, 1969, which was over in three hours.

The perfunctory trial, while it may not have represented a miscarriage of justice, was an unsatisfying resolution to a national tragedy. It left a bad taste in many mouths.

Conspiracy theories have found many advocates in the years since the assassination, fueled by Ray's repeated assertions that he was not guilty, that he was manipulated by Raoul and others. Those who believe in a cover-up usually cite the hostility toward King of J. Edgar Hoover, whose use of FBI power in relation to King, as documented by the House and Senate Reports on Assassinations in the late 1970s, sometimes crossed the line between investigation and harassment.

(see FBI, HOOVER)

B

BACKLASH

The guardians of the status quo lash out with denunciation against the person or organization they consider most responsible for the emergence of the new order. Often this denunciation rises to major proportions. In the transition from slavery to restricted emancipation Abraham Lincoln was assassinated.

—*Stride Toward Freedom*, p. 193
(SEE ASSASSINATION)

BANKRUPTCY

A civilization can founder as readily in the face of moral and spiritual bankruptcy as it can through financial bankruptcy.

—*Where Do We Go from Here?* p. 186

BAPTISM

Martin Luther King was baptized in 1934 at the age of five. It occurred during a sermon by a guest minister at Ebenezer Baptist Church who made a persuasive call for the salvation of budding young souls.

Martin's older sister Christine King, then age six, stood up and answered the call. Martin, who later admitted that he was competing with Christine throughout his childhood, followed suit immediately.

"I decided that I would not let her get ahead of me, so I was the next."

BEAUTY

Our children must be taught to stand tall with their heads proudly lifted. We need not be duped into purchasing bleaching creams that make us lighter. We need not process our hair to make it appear straight. Whether some men, black or white, realize it or not, black people are very beautiful.

—*Where Do We Go from Here?* p. 123
(see SELF-ESTEEM)

BELOVED COMMUNITY

When the Montgomery Bus Boycott ended in triumph for Dr. King and the black people of Montgomery, Alabama, he spoke at a victory rally on December 3, 1956. The goal was not to defeat the white man, he said, but to awaken the white man's conscience and to challenge his false sense of superiority.

Now that victory had been achieved in Montgomery, said Dr. King, it was time for reconciliation. "The end is reconciliation; the end is redemption; the end is the creation of the beloved community."

A recurring theme in King's sermons, from the beginning of his career to the end, was what he called the Beloved Community. It was the ultimate goal for which he worked. The Beloved Community was an integrated community in which all men and women of all races and creeds lived together harmoniously as brothers and sisters in peace. It was the Kingdom of God come to earth.

I do not think of political power as an end. Neither do I think of economic power as an end. They are ingredients in the objective that we seek in life. And I think that end or that objective is a truly brotherly society, the creation of the beloved community.

—*Christian Century*, July 13, 1966

The Negro saw that by proving the sweeping and majestic power of nonviolence to bring about the beloved community, it might be possible for him to set an example to a whole world caught up in conflict.

—*Why We Can't Wait*, p. 45
(see CHRISTIAN LOVE, HEAVEN, KINGDOM OF GOD, LOVE, RECONCILIATION)

BIG WORDS

As a young boy, Martin Luther King liked to listen to preachers. One time, at age ten, he asked his father to take him to see a well-known preacher, who was giving a guest sermon at another church. His father obliged.

Young King was impressed by the sermon. "Daddy," he said, "that man had some big words. When I grow up I'm going to get me some big words."

His father recalled: "As soon as he could read, he lived in dictionaries, and he made that saying come true. He got himself some big words."

BILL OF RIGHTS FOR THE DISADVANTAGED

King proposed a Bill of Rights for the Disadvantaged, including poor people of all races.

"I am proposing," he wrote in *Why We Can't Wait*, "that, just as we granted a GI Bill of Rights to war veterans, America launch a broad-based and gigantic Bill of Rights for the Disadvantaged, our veterans of the long siege of denial."

The bill would provide not only for equal opportunity but for the training that would enable the disadvantaged to take advantage of equal opportunity. "The struggle for rights is, at bottom, a struggle for opportunities," he said. "With equal opportunity must come the practical, realistic aid which will equip him to seize it. Giving a pair of shoes to a man who has not learned to walk is a cruel jest."

A Bill of Rights for the Disadvantaged could mark the rise of a new era, in which the full resources of the society would be used to attack the tenacious poverty which so paradoxically exists in the midst of plenty.

—*Why We Can't Wait*, pp. 138–39
(see GUARANTEED NATIONAL INCOME)

BIRMINGHAM

"Nonviolence had passed the test of its steel in the fires of turmoil," wrote King in *Why We Can't Wait*. "The united power of southern segregation was the hammer. Birmingham was the anvil."

If Montgomery in 1955 was the first battle in the war to desegregate the South, Birmingham in 1963 was the turning point in that war. It was a long, hard-fought campaign.

"Here was a city which had been trapped for decades in a Rip Van Winkle slumber, a city whose fathers had apparently never heard of Abraham Lincoln, Thomas Jefferson, the Preamble to the Constitution, the Thirteenth, Four-teenth and Fifteenth Amendments, or the 1954 Supreme Court decision outlawing segregation in the public schools."

The campaign to desegregate Birmingham, Alabama, began losing momentum as days dragged on. There was disagreement among the leaders meeting at the Gaston Hotel. Should King stick to his original plan of subjecting himself to arrest, in the hope of drawing national attention to the struggle? Worried colleagues advised him against it.

"Martin, you can't go to jail now. We need you to raise money. You're the only one who can do it," said one.

"We're almost broke. And without bail money, the dem-onstrators who go to jail will have to stay there," said an-other.

"And if we can't promise bail, it'll be hard to find new volunteers for demonstrations," cautioned another.

King sighed and remained silent for a long time. He wrote about this moment later: "There comes a time when a leader, even though he may be surrounded by loyal friends and allies, still has to come face to face with him-self. I was alone in that crowded room."

King rose to leave the meeting. "I need to be alone now for awhile. I'll let you know my decision." He walked into another room in the back of the suite and prayed for an answer. A few minutes later he returned. He was wearing his dungarees. He had decided to go to jail.

"I don't know what will happen," he said. "I don't know where the money will come from. But I have to make a faith act."

As the demonstration approached the downtown area, he walked toward the police barricade.

Ralph Abernathy ran to join him. "I'm coming with you, Martin."

The two pastors reached the police barricade and stood

face to face with a glowering Police Commissioner Bull Connor.

King dropped to his knees in prayer. Abernathy did the same.

Connor circled, swinging his nightstick. He signaled his men.

"Arrest 'em. Demonstratin' without a permit."

Policemen seized King and Abernathy by the seats of their pants and shoved them into a paddy wagon. They were taken to Birmingham City Jail, where King would be placed in solitary confinement in a cell without a mattress or a blanket and barred from communicating with the outside world.

Abernathy and King did not know how long they would be in the Birmingham jail. They did not know what was in store for them as the doors of the paddy wagon shut.

At that moment King turned to Abernathy and said, "Do you remember what day this is, Ralph?"

Abernathy nodded. "Yes. It's Good Friday."

(see Biography 1963, BIRMINGHAM JAIL,
LETTER FROM BIRMINGHAM JAIL)

BIRMINGHAM JAIL

The day after Easter, 1963, the phone rang at the King house. Coretta King, who had not heard from her husband since his arrest in Birmingham on Friday, ran to pick up the receiver.

Her two-year-old son Dexter grabbed it first. He was babbling cheerfully into the receiver in the living room when she came on the line in the kitchen.

A White House operator spoke. "Will you get your child off the phone, please?"

Coretta instructed someone to retrieve the other phone from Dexter. Then President Kennedy's familiar Boston accent was heard on the other end. JFK was calling from Hyannisport, returning her call from the day before.

"Mrs. King, I'm sorry I wasn't able to talk to you yesterday. I just wanted you to know that I was with my father. He just had a stroke, and I couldn't leave him."

"I'm very sorry about your father."

"How are you, Mrs. King? I understand you have a new baby."

"I'm fine and the baby's fine," said Coretta. "But I'm concerned about my husband in Birmingham jail."

"We checked on your husband and he's all right. I want you to know we're doing everything we can. Of course, Birmingham is a difficult place. But I've just talked to them and your husband will be calling you shortly."

The President told her if she had any further worries about her husband to call him again. Almost as soon as she hung up the phone it rang again. It was Martin calling from Birmingham City Jail. They had finally allowed him to use the telephone. "Corrie?"

"Are you all right, Martin?"

He sounded tired and weak. "I'm all right."

"President Kennedy just called. He said he's spoken with someone there."

"So that's why everybody is suddenly being so polite." Martin began to perk up. "Corrie, I want you to tell Wyatt Walker about the President's call. Tell him I want him to make a statement to the press. It might give us a boost."

After President Kennedy's call to Birmingham City Jail, King was given a mattress and a blanket and allowed to communicate with the outside world once again. He resumed active leadership of the campaign from his jail cell.

Monday, April 16, the day of President Kennedy's call, proved to be a turning point in the Birmingham campaign. The Birmingham officials began to realize that the President—and indeed, the entire nation—was watching.

25

That was the day Martin Luther King commenced writing his immortal Letter from Birmingham Jail.

(see KENNEDY, JOHN F., LETTER FROM BIRMINGHAM JAIL)

BITTERNESS

Never succumb to the temptation of bitterness.

—*The Strength to Love*, p. 131

The one thing about bitterness is its blindness. Bitterness has not the capacity to make the distinction between some and *all*.

—*Where Do We Go From Here?* p. 26
(see FEAR, HATRED, HOPE, NEGATIVE FREEDOM)

BLACK AND WHITE

"We are not going to allow this conflict in Birmingham to deteriorate into a struggle between black people and white people," declared Dr. King at a mass meeting on May 15, 1963. "The tension in Birmingham is between justice and injustice."

Immediately after the Birmingham settlement was reached, and the demonstrators' demands had been agreed to by the merchants, there was a backlash of violence from white racists. The Ku Klux Klan bombed several churches, including the church of King's younger brother, A. D. King. The motel room where King and Abernathy were staying was also bombed.

Unhurt, King announced to a crowd that there had also been a drive-by shooting of a young black man by a white motorist. When voices were raised in anger, King held up his hand. "I'm sorry, but I will *never* teach any of you to hate white people."

* * *

There is no separate black path to power and fulfillment that does not intersect white paths, and there is no separate white path to power and fulfillment, short of social disaster, that does not share that power with black aspirations for freedom and human dignity. We are bound together in a single garment of destiny.

—*Where Do We Go from Here?* p. 52

BLACK CONSCIOUSNESS

To develop a sense of black consciousness and peoplehood does not require that we scorn the white race as a whole. It is not the race per se that we fight but the policies and ideology that leaders of that race have formulated to perpetuate oppression.

—*The Trumpet of Conscience*, p. 9
(see BLACK AND WHITE, WHITE)

BLACK FAMILY

In the 1960s the first national alarms were sounded about the problem of the disintegration of the black family structure in the ghetto. In 1965 the Moynihan Report, sponsored by the Johnson White House, with contributions from many academic leaders including Kenneth Clark, Talcott Parsons, Eric Erickson, Robert Coles, and James Wilson, presented a disturbing picture of a fatherless family pattern emerging in black poverty.

In a speech in Westchester County, New York, in October 1965, King expressed his provisional approval of the Moynihan Report. But he had one major reservation: "The danger will be that problems will be attributed to innate Negro weaknesses and used to justify neglect and rationalize oppression."

(see CHILDREN, FAMILY, GHETTO)

"I pleaded with the group to abandon the Black Power slogan," recalled Dr. King of a meeting with Stokely Carmichael and other militant black leaders in Yazoo, Mississippi, in 1966. "It was my contention that a leader has to be concerned about the problem of semantics. Each word, I said, has a denotative meaning : . . . and a connotative meaning. . . . Black Power carried the wrong connotations."

Stokely Carmichael snapped back: "Power is the only thing respected in this world, and we must get it at any cost."

The unity of the black freedom movement characterized by the early years of King's leadership from 1956 to 1963 was a thing of the past by the mid-sixties. The freedom movement became increasingly polarized, along with the rest of American society, during the Vietnam era.

The rise of the Black Power movement within the civil rights movement marked the beginning of Martin Luther King's decline in influence. Although the effectiveness of the militant black power strategy was still unproven, for many young people the message had an emotional appeal equal to or greater than King's nonviolent direct action strategy. During the Selma march, some of the young blacks began substituting the lyric, "We shall overrun" for "We Shall Overcome."

King was disturbed to hear lyrics such as these:

> Jingle bells, shotgun shells,
> Freedom all the way,
> Oh what fun it is to blast
> A trooper man away.

The mood was shifting from nonviolence toward violence. A new generation of black leaders, such as Stokely

Carmichael and H. Rap Brown, arose to compete with Dr. King. Riots were replacing demonstrations as the popular means of expressing protest.

"The white man is your enemy," declared Brown in the summer of 1967. "You got to destroy your enemy . . . I say you better get a gun. Violence is necessary—it is as American as cherry pie."

King continued to insist that nonviolence was the only way to successfully revolutionize America.

We can't win violently. We have neither the instruments nor the techniques at our disposal, and it would be totally absurd for us to believe we could do it.

—Speech, Yazoo, Mississippi, June 26, 1966

Beneath all the satisfaction of a gratifying slogan, Black Power is a nihilistic philosophy born out of the conviction that the Negro can't win. It was born from the wounds of despair and disappointment.

—*Where Do We Go from Here?* p. 44

In the final analysis, the weakness of black power is its failure to see that the black man needs the white man and the white man needs the black man.

—*Where Do We Go from Here?* p. 52
(see BLACK AND WHITE, DIVISION, REVOLUTION, WHITE)

BLACK SUPREMACY

We must not become victimized with a philosophy of black supremacy. God is not interested merely in the freedom of black men, and brown men, and yellow men; God is interested in the freedom of the whole human race.

—*Stride Toward Freedom*, p. 221

BOMBING

At 9:15 p.m. on January 30, 1956, Coretta King and a friend were conversing in the living room when they heard the thump of an object tossed on the front porch of the King home. They jumped up and hurried toward the bedroom in the rear of the house where the baby Yolanda was sleeping. Moments later the house shook with the explosion of a homemade bomb. Glass and flame spilled into the room they had just vacated.

Soon after the phone rang and Coretta answered it. "Yes, I did it," snorted a nasal female voice. "And I'm just sorry I didn't kill all you bastards."

Dr. King, who was meeting with a church group about the Montgomery Bus Boycott, then in its second month, was notified of what had happened. He rushed home and found his house surrounded by more than three hundred blacks, many of them armed and angry.

Once he was reassured that Coretta and the baby were safe, he returned to his front porch. Policemen were trying to disband the crowd. One man shouted furiously: "You white folks is always pushin' us around. Now you got your .38 and I got mine, so let's battle it out." The crowd was getting unruly. King stepped onto his smouldering porch and called for quiet.

"We believe in law and order," he said. "Don't get your weapons. Remember the words of Jesus. He who lives by the sword will perish by the sword. We are not advocating violence. We want to love our enemies. We must love our white brothers no matter what they do to us. We must make them know that we love them."

He stood on his porch and calmed the crowd with his soft, strong words. He spoke like a prophet.

"We cannot solve this problem through retaliatory violence. We must meet violence with nonviolence. . . . We must meet hate with love."

The restless men set down their bats, put away their knives and other weapons, and with King's words echoing in their minds, they peacefully dispersed, turning their steps toward home.

(see NONVIOLENCE, RETALIATION)

BOTTOM

Dr. King and Ralph Abernathy were arrested together for leading a protest in Albany, Georgia, and sentenced to forty-five days in jail. They were taken to a tiny concrete cell with two bunks and a filthy commode.

Glancing at the double-decker bunk bed, Abernathy said, "Do you want the top or the bottom?"

"I don't want either," said King, folding his arms.

"I'll take the top," said Abernathy. "It's further away from the commode."

King reflected for a moment and said, "I'll take the bottom."

(see SNORE)

BROTHERHOOD

After the March from Selma to Montgomery in the spring of 1966, there was a delay at the airport and several thousand people had to wait for their planes. As he watched the crowd, King was struck by the heterogeneity of the crowd and at the same time by the unity of its members. He made this observation:

"As I stood with them and saw white and Negro, nuns and priests, ministers and rabbis, labor organizers, lawyers, doctors, housemaids and shopworkers brimming with vitality and enjoying a rare comradeship, I knew I was seeing a microcosm of the mankind of the future in this moment of luminous and genuine brotherhood."

One of Martin Luther King's fundamental principles was the brotherhood of man. He believed all life is part of a single process; all living things are interrelated; and all men and women are brothers and sisters. Whites and blacks are brothers in the brotherhood of man. All have a place in the Beloved Community. Because all are interrelated one cannot harm another person without harming oneself.

Man is a child of God, made in His image, and therefore must be respected as such. Until men see this everywhere, until nations see this everywhere, we will be fighting wars. One day somebody should remind us that, even though there may be political and ideological differences between us, the Vietnamese are our brothers, the Russians are our brothers, the Chinese are our brothers; and one day we've got to sit down at the table of brotherhood.

—*The Trumpet of Conscience*, p. 72

We are inevitably our brother's keeper because we are our brother's brother.

—*Where Do We Go from Here?* p. 181
(see INTERDEPENDENCE, WORLD PERSPECTIVE)

BRUTALITY

I am expert in recognition of a simple eloquent truth. That truth is that it is sinful to brutalize any of God's other children, no matter from what side the brutalization comes.

—Article, "Peace: God's Man's Business," *Chicago Defender*, January 1–7, 1966
(see HATRED, RETALIATION, VIOLENCE, WAR)

C

CADILLACS

When the news reached King's supporters that he was to be released from Birmingham City Jail after the intervention of the Kennedy White House in April 1963, it was hailed as a great victory for the Birmingham campaign. King's followers immediately made plans to honor him with a Cadillac motorcade on his way home from prison. When Coretta visited him in jail before his release and told him of this plan, King immediately vetoed it.

"No," he said, shaking his head. "Tell them no."

"Martin, you're a hero to these people," said Coretta. "They want to honor you."

"What we're doing here is a spiritual movement first and foremost. Now what would I look like coming back from jail in a Cadillac? You just drive our car to the airport and I'll drive home."

Coretta was disappointed because she knew the others would be disappointed.

"Are you sure?" she asked.

"Jesus would have walked home from jail," said Martin with a grin.

"Jesus didn't have a car," said Coretta. "We do."

"We have a Ford," replied Martin, "not a Cadillac."

CAPITALISM

Truth is not to be found either in traditional capitalism or in Marxism. Each represents a partial truth. Historically, capitalism failed to discern the truth in collective enterprise and Marxism failed to see the truth in individual enterprise.

—*The Strength to Love*, pp. 98–99

Nineteenth-century capitalism failed to appreciate that life is social, and Marxism failed ... to see that life is individual and social. The Kingdom of God is neither the thesis of individual enterprise nor the antithesis of collective enterprise, but a synthesis which reconciles the truth of both.

—*The Strength to Love*, p. 99

The profit motive, when it is the sole basis of an economic system, encourages a cutthroat competition and selfish ambition that inspires men to be more concerned about making a living than making a life.

—*The Strength to Love*, p. 98

Capitalism may lead to a practical materialism that is as pernicious as the theoretical materialism taught by communism.

—*The Strength to Love*, p. 98
(see COMMUNISM, DIALECTICISM, MAN, SYNTHESIS)

CAR WASH

Daddy King was more frugal than his son. The senior King even insisted on washing his own car. "You should wash it yourself," he said to Martin Luther King, Jr., who preferred the luxury of a car wash.

"Daddy, I have a theory about that," replied his son the young philosopher. "Society is based on division of labor, you see, and if I wash my own car it means somebody else doesn't have a job. So I'm doing my part to alleviate unemployment."

(see UNEMPLOYMENT)

CHALLENGE

The ultimate measure of a man is not where he stands in moments of comfort and convenience, but where he stands at times of challenge and controversy.

—*The Strength to Love*, p. 20

CHAOS

If the American Negro and other victims of oppression succumb to the temptation of using violence in the struggle for freedom, future generations will be the recipients of a desolate night of bitterness, and our chief legacy to them will be an endless reign of meaningless chaos.

—*Stride Toward Freedom*, p. 213

The white society, unprepared and unwilling to accept radical structural change, is resisting firmly and thus producing chaos because the force for change is vital and aggressive. The irony is that the white society ruefully

35

complains that if there were no chaos great changes would come, yet it creates the circumstances breeding the chaos.

—The Trumpet of Conscience, p. 9
(see CHOICE, REVOLUTION)

CHILDREN

Thousands of children participated in the Birmingham protests during the spring of 1963. Hundreds were arrested. Criticized for using children in his demonstrations, King offered this defense of the strategy:

"A hundred times I have been asked why we have allowed little children to march in demonstrations, to freeze and suffer in jails, to be exposed to bullets and dynamite. The questions imply that we have revealed a want of family feeling or a recklessness toward family security. The answer is simple. Our children and our families are maimed a little every day of our lives. If we can end an incessant torture by a single climactic confrontation, the risks are acceptable. Moreover, our family life will be born anew if we fight together.

"Other families may be fortunate enough to be able to protect their young from danger. Our families, as we have seen, are different. Oppression has again and again divided and splintered them. We are a people torn apart from era to era. It is logical, moral, and psychologically constructive for us to resist oppression united as families. Out of this unity, out of the bond of fighting together, forges will come. The inner strength and integrity will make us whole again."

At a mass meeting in Birmingham on May 3, 1963, King addressed the parents of the children. "Now, finally, your children, your daughters and sons are in jail, many of them, and I'm sure many of the parents are here tonight." He paused and then spoke with a reassuring calmness: "Don't worry about them. They are suffering for what they believe, and they are suffering to make this nation a better nation."

(see BLACK FAMILY, FAMILY)

CHOICE

In a world in which evil arises from the wrong choices human beings make with their God-given gift of free will, making the right choices is what makes all the difference. Ultimately we must choose, said Martin Luther King, between nonviolence and violence, between peace and war, between good and evil. And not only must we choose, but we must choose before it is too late. We must choose while we still have a choice.

"We still have a choice today," he stated in the conclusion of his last book, *Where Do We Go from Here: Chaos or Community?*, "nonviolent coexistence or violent coannihilation. This may well be mankind's last chance to choose between chaos and community."

(see CHAOS)

CHRIST

He knew that the old eye-for-an-eye philosophy would leave everyone blind. He did not seek to overcome evil with evil. He overcame evil with good. Although crucified by hate, he responded with aggressive love.

—*The Strength to Love*, p. 28

In Christ there is neither Jew nor Gentile. In Christ there is neither male nor female. In Christ there is neither Communist nor capitalist. In Christ, somehow, there is neither bound nor free. We are all one in Jesus Christ. And when we truly believe in the sacredness of human personality,

we won't exploit people, we won't trample over people
with the iron feet of oppression, we won't kill anybody.

—*The Trumpet of Conscience*, p. 72

Christ came to show us the way. Men love darkness rather
than the light, and they crucified Him, and there on Good
Friday on the Cross it was still dark, but then Easter came,
and Easter is an eternal reminder of the fact that the truth-
crushed earth will rise again.

—*The Trumpet of Conscience*, p. 75

We will return good for evil. We will love our enemies.
Christ showed us the way and Gandhi showed us it could
work.

—Sermon at Riverside Church in New York, April 4, 1967
(see GANDHI, NONVIOLENCE)

CHRISTIAN FAITH

Love is one of the pinnacle parts of the Christian faith.
There is another side called justice. And justice is really
love in calculation.

—Speech, Montgomery, Alabama, December 5, 1955

CHRISTIAN GOSPEL

The Christian Gospel is a two-way road. On the one hand,
it seeks to change the souls of men and thereby unite them
with God; on the other hand, it seeks to change the envi-
ronmental conditions of men so that the soul will have a
chance after it is changed.

—*Stride Toward Freedom*, p. 36
(see RELIGION)

CHRISTIANITY

Napoleon Bonaparte, the great military genius, looking back over his years of conquest, is reported to have said: "Alexander, Caesar, Charlemagne and I have built great empires. But upon what did they depend? They depended on force. But centuries ago Jesus started an empire that was built on love, and even to this day millions would die for him."

—*The Strength to Love*, p. 41

We are gravely mistaken to think that religion protects us from the pain and agony of mortal existence. Life is not a euphoria of unalloyed comfort and untroubled ease. Christianity has always insisted that the cross we bear precedes the crown we wear.

—Sermon, "Beyond Discovery, Love," Dallas, Texas, September 25, 1966

To be a Christian one must take up his cross, with all of its difficulties and agonizing and tension-packed content and carry it until that very cross leaves its marks upon us and redeems us to that more excellent way which comes only through suffering.

—Speech, Chicago, January 17, 1963

When I took up the cross, I recognized its meaning. . . . The cross is something that you bear, and ultimately that you die on.

—Speech, Penn Community Center, Frogmore, South Carolina, May 22, 1967

Christianity clearly affirms that in the long struggle between good and evil, good eventually will emerge as victor.

—*The Strength to Love*, p. 59

CHRISTIAN LOVE

"From the beginning a basic philosophy guided the movement," wrote King in *Stride Toward Freedom: The Montgomery Story.* "This guiding principle has since been referred to variously as nonviolent resistance, noncooperation, and passive resistance. But in the first days of the protest none of these expressions was mentioned; the phrase most often heard was 'Christian love.' It was the Sermon on the Mount, rather than a doctrine of passive resistance, that initially inspired the Negroes of Montgomery to dignified social action. It was Jesus of Nazareth that stirred the Negroes to protest with the creative weapon of love."

The command to love one's enemy is an absolute necessity for our survival. Love even for enemies is the key to the solution of problems of our world. Jesus is not an impractical idealist; he is the practical realist.

—*The Strength to Love*, p. 34
(see FORGIVENESS, LOVE, NONCOOPERATION)

CHURCH

If today's church does not recapture the sacrificial spirit of the early church, it will lose its authenticity, forfeit the loyalty of millions, and be dismissed as an irrelevant social club.

—Letter from Birmingham Jail, 1963
(see RELIGION)

CITIES

Most of the largest cities are victims of the large migration of Negroes. Although it was well known that millions of Negroes would be forced off the land in the South by the contraction of agricultural employment during the past two decades, no national planning was done to provide remedies. When white immigrants arrived in the United States in the late nineteenth century, a beneficent government gave them free land and credit to build a useful, independent life. In contrast, when the Negro migrated, he was left to his own resources. He crowded the cities and was herded into ghettos, left in unemployment, or subjected to gross exploitation within a context of searing discrimination.

—*The Trumpet of Conscience*, p. 12
(see ECONOMIC INJUSTICE, POVERTY)

CIVIL DISOBEDIENCE

King considered mass civil disobedience the next step in nonviolent revolution after mass protest. Civil disobedience not only transforms the legal system—it transforms the activist who practices it. "Words cannot express the exultation," remarked King, "felt by the individual as he finds himself, with hundreds of his fellows, behind prison bars for a cause he knows is just."

An individual who breaks a law that conscience tells him is unjust, and who willingly accepts the penalty of imprisonment in order to arouse the conscience of the community over its injustice, is in reality expressing the highest respect for law.

—Letter from Birmingham Jail, 1963

In no sense do I advocate evading or defying the law, as would the rabid segregationist. That would lead to anarchy. One who breaks an unjust law must do so openly, lovingly, and with a willingness to accept the penalty.

—Letter from Birmingham Jail, 1963

There is nothing new about this kind of civil disobedience. . . . It was practiced superbly by the early Christians, who were willing to face hungry lions and the excruciating pain of chopping blocks rather than submit to certain unjust laws of the Roman Empire. To a degree, academic freedom is a reality because Socrates practiced civil disobedience. In our own nation, the Boston Tea Party represented a massive act of civil disobedience.

—Letter from Birmingham Jail, 1963

Never forget that everything that Hitler did in Germany was legal. It was illegal to aid and comfort a Jew in the day of Hitler's Germany. And I believe if I had lived there with my present attitude I would have disobeyed that law, and I would have encouraged people to aid and comfort our Jewish brothers.

—Speech, "True Peace," Atlanta, July 5, 1962

To raise protest to an appropriate level for cities, it is necessary to adopt civil disobedience. To dislocate the functioning of a city, without destroying it, can be more effective than a riot because it can be longer lasting, costly to the society, but not wantonly destructive.

—Speech, "The Crisis in American Cities," August 15, 1967

If a people can produce from its ranks 5 percent who will go voluntarily to jail for a just cause, surely nothing can thwart its ultimate triumph.

—Why We Can't Wait, p. 44

(see LAW, LETTER FROM BIRMINGHAM JAIL, PROTEST, REVOLUTION)

CIVIL RIGHTS

"The collective effort that was born out of the civil rights alliance was awesomely fruitful for this country in the first years of the 1960s. The repressive forces that had not been seriously challenged for almost a decade now faced an aroused adversary. A torrent of humanist thought and action swept across the land, scoring first small and then larger victories. The awakening grew in breadth, and the contested issues encompassed other social questions. A phalanx of reliable young activists took protest from hiding and revived a sense of responsible rebellion. A peace movement was born."

This was Dr. King's overview of the triumphant period of the civil rights movement, as expressed in a 1967 lecture, "Youth and Social Action."

Before the end of his life, King saw the civil rights movement break up into factions. He realized that the first phase of the civil rights movement—which he called the "protest" phase—was over.

"There is a sense in which it can be said that the civil rights and peace movements are over—at least in their first form, the protest form, which gave them their first victories. There is a sense in which the alliance of responsible young people which the movement represented has fallen apart under the impact of failures, discouragement, and consequent extremism and polarization. The movement for social change has entered a time of temptation to despair because it is clear now how deep and systematic are the evils it confronts."

King did not live long enough to lead the civil rights movement into its next phase. He envisioned an expanded human rights movement, international in scope, broad enough to include poor people of all races, and based on the principles of nonviolent resistance. "As the young people face this crisis, leaders in the movement are working out programs to bring the social movements through from their early, and now inadequate, protest phase to a new stage of massive, active, nonviolent resistance to the evils of the modern system."

* * *

More and more, the civil rights movement will have to engage in the task of organizing people into permanent groups to protect their own interests and produce change in their behalf. This task is tedious, and lacks the drama of demonstrations, but it is necessary for meaningful results.

—*Where Do We Go from Here?* p. 131

The revolution for human rights is opening up unhealthy areas in American life and permitting a new and wholesome healing to take place. Eventually the civil rights movement will have contributed infinitely more to the nation than the eradication of racial injustice. It will have enlarged the concept of brotherhood to a vision of total interrelatedness. . . . In measuring the full implications of the civil rights revolution, the greatest contribution may be in the area of world peace.

—Conclusion of *Why We Can't Wait*, p. 152
(see GROUP, ORGANIZATION, PEACE)

COMMITMENT

"We've got to learn that a man's worth is not measured by his bank account or the size of the wheelbase of his car. It is measured by his commitment."

In the self-eulogy delivered by King on February 4, 1968, two months before his death, he talked about what he would leave behind when he was dead.

"I won't have any money to leave behind. I won't have the fine and luxurious things of life to leave behind. But I just want to leave a committed life behind."

COMMUNISM

Martin Luther King was called a communist by J. Edgar Hoover. It would be interesting to know whether Hoover, or anyone in the FBI, ever read what King had to say about communism in his book *Stride Toward Freedom*. King's rejection of communism is thoughtful and compelling: "In communism the individual ends up in subjection to the state," he wrote. "Man becomes hardly more, in communism, than a depersonalized cog in the turning wheel of the state."

The popularity of communism, King asserted, lay in its idealistic concern for social justice. "With all its false assumptions and evil methods, communism grew as a protest against the hardships of the underprivileged. Communism in theory emphasized a classless society, and a concern for social justice, though the world knows from sad experience that in practice it created new classes and a new lexicon of injustice."

Communism would never be defeated by military opposition, in King's view. Communism would be defeated by a change in values. The defeat of communism would be moral and mental, not military.

"Positive revolution of values is our best defense against communism," King said in a sermon at Riverside Church on April 4, 1967. "War is not the answer. Communism will never be defeated by the use of atomic bombs or nuclear weapons."

Communism and Christianity are fundamentally incompatible. A true Christian cannot be a true communist, for the two philosophies are antithetical and all the dialectics of the logicians cannot reconcile them.

—*The Strength to Love*, p. 93

Nothing provides the communists with a better climate for expansion and infiltration than the continued alliance of our nation with racism and exploitation throughout the world.

—*Where Do We Go from Here?* p. 174

Cold atheism wrapped in the garments of materialism, communism provides no place for God or Christ.

—*The Strength to Love*, p. 94

Since for the communist there is no divine government, no absolute moral order, there are no fixed, immutable principles; consequently almost anything—force, violence, murder, lying—is a justifiable means to the "millennial" end.... Constructive ends can never give absolute moral justification to destructive means, because in the final analysis the end is preexistent in the mean.

—*Stride Toward Freedom*, p. 92

Our irrational, obsessive anti-communism has led us into too many quagmires.

—Speech, Carnegie Hall, New York, February 23, 1968

We must not engage in a negative anti-communism, but rather in a positive thrust for democracy, realizing that our greatest defense against communism is to take offensive action on behalf of justice and righteousness.

—*The Strength to Love*, p. 100

Communism thrives only when the doors of opportunity are closed and human aspirations are stifled.

—*The Strength to Love*, p. 100

Communism is a judgment on our failure to make democracy real and to follow through on the revolutions we initiated.

—*Where Do We Go from Here?* p. 190

Is communism alive in the world today because we have not been Christian enough?

—*The Strength to Love*, p. 99
(see CAPITALISM, DIALECTICAL METHOD, MAN)

COMMUNISTS

On June 22, 1963, President Kennedy met with Dr. King and a group of civil rights leaders at the White House. After the meeting adjourned, the President asked King to stay behind. In order to avoid having their conversation bugged by Hoover or any other unwanted listeners, President Kennedy took King for a walk in the Rose Garden.

In the Rose Garden President Kennedy put his hand on King's shoulder and told him he must "get rid of" Stanley Levison and Jack O'Dell—two of King's closest white associates.

"They're communists," said JFK.

The FBI had been warning the Kennedy administration to disassociate itself from King in case it was publicly exposed that King was under communist influence.

King answered: "Communists? I'm not quite sure what that means, Mr. President. Hoover considers a great many people communists. He probably considers me a communist, and I am not a communist."

JFK confided that, according to information from the FBI, O'Dell was the "number five communist" in the United States and Stanley Levison was his "handler."

King did not take this allegation very seriously. "I don't see how O'Dell's got time to do all that," he said with a chuckle. "He's got two jobs with me."

President Kennedy was not amused. He warned of a potential scandal that could ruin the chances of his civil rights bill. "If they shoot you down," said JFK, "they'll shoot us down."

King was torn between his desire to support the President's civil rights bill and his personal loyalty to his friends, especially Levison.

"Mr. President, I can't believe Stanley Levison is a communist," King said firmly, "and I won't believe it until I see proof."

Satisfactory proof never materialized. At a press conference on July 17, President Kennedy announced there was "no evidence" to show that any civil rights leaders were communists. "I think it is a convenient scapegoat," said the president, "to suggest that all the difficulties are communist."

(see HOOVER, LEVISON)

COMMUNITY

The "most creative turn of events" in man's long history occurred when man set down his stone ax and began to cooperate with his neighbor. "That seemingly elementary decision set in motion what we know now as civilization," King wrote in a 1963 article titled "The Ethical Demands of Integration." At the heart of all that civilization has meant and developed is 'community'—the mutually cooperative and voluntary venture of man to assume a semblance of responsibility for his brother."

The cross is the eternal expression of the length to which God will go in order to restore broken community. The resurrection is a symbol of God's triumph over all the forces that seek to block community. The Holy Spirit is the continuing community creating reality that moves through history.

—Stride Toward Freedom, p. 105–6
(see BELOVED COMMUNITY)

COMPASSION

Here is the true meaning of compassion and nonviolence, when they help us to see the enemy's point of view, to hear his questions, to know his assessment of ourselves. For from his view we may indeed see the basic weakness of our condition, and if we are mature, we may learn and grow and profit from the wisdom of the brothers who are called the opposition.

—*The Trumpet of Conscience*, p. 29
(see LOVE, NONVIOLENCE, RECONCILIATION)

CONFORMIST

Most people, and Christians in particular, are thermometers that record or register the temperature of majority of opinion, not thermostats that transform or regulate the temperature of society.

—*The Strength to Love*, p. 10
(see NONCONFORMIST)

CONSCIENCE

King sought to transform society by appealing to the conscience of those who, knowingly or unknowingly, perpetuated injustice. His goal was to awaken the sleeping conscience of America.

"Nonviolence can touch men where the law cannot reach them," he wrote in *Stride Toward Freedom*. "It is the method which seeks to implement the just law by appealing to the consciences of the great decent majority who through blindness, fear, pride, or irrationality have allowed their consciences to sleep."

COOLING OFF

Emotions were running high on May 20, 1961, when Attorney General Robert Kennedy sent seven hundred federal marshals to Montgomery, Alabama, to rescue Dr. King and his congregation from a riotous mob of racists who had surrounded the First Baptist Church. After the smoke cleared, the Attorney General asked for a "cooling off" period at the end of May; in other words, a temporary suspension of demonstrations.

King publicly rebuffed this White House request. "We have been cooling off for one hundred years," he retorted. "This is no time to engage in the luxury of cooling off or to take the tranquilizing drug of gradualism. Now is the time to make real the promises of democracy."

However, instead of a cooling off, King did agree to a "temporary lull." It was a typical example of King's careful use of semantics. Thus he avoided the impression of colluding with, or conceding to, the Kennedy White House, while at the same time avoiding alienating Robert Kennedy, who proved to be one of his strongest allies in the establishment.

(see BLACK POWER, LAW)

CORETTA SCOTT

"Mary, I wish I knew a few girls from down home to go out with," remarked Martin, a doctoral student at Boston University, to Mrs. Mary Powell, an Atlantan residing in Boston. "I tell you, these Boston girls are something else. The ones I've been seeing are so reserved."

Mrs. Powell immediately thought of Coretta Scott, a graduate of Antioch College and the daughter of a prosperous storekeeper from Marion, Alabama, who was studying voice at the New England Conservatory of Music. He politely demanded her telephone number.

Martin called Coretta Scott a few days later. He tried to charm her with his seductive baritone and his sophisticated Don Juan manner over the telephone.

"I am like Napoleon at Waterloo before your charms," said the young lothario into the receiver. "I'm on my knees."

That line might have been effective with some of Martin's previous romantic conquests, but its effect on Coretta was to produce laughter.

"Why, that's absurd," she said. "You haven't seen me yet."

Once Martin did see her, it didn't take him long to make up his mind that she was the woman for him. He proposed to her on their first date.

The next time Martin saw Mary Powell at the Conservatory he had Coretta Scott on his arm. "Mary," he said with a wink, "I owe you a thousand dollars for introducing me to this girl."

"I'll take it," said Mary Powell, smiling.

"Mary," said Martin graciously, "I'll always owe you a thousand dollars for introducing me to this girl."

(see FIRST DATE, HONEYMOON)

COURAGE

King received thousands of death threats during the fourteen years of his leadership of the civil rights movement. Because he advocated nonviolence, he was often accused of being a coward. But nothing could be further from the truth. It takes extraordinary courage to stand up, unarmed, against the armed forces of bigotry and hatred.

King was subjected to two bombings, one nearly fatal knife attack, and countless death threats by mail and telephone. He was hit by police billy clubs; he was struck in the head by thrown stones; he was punched by Ku Klux

Klanners; he was spied upon by FBI agents; and he always knew that he was an easy target for a sniper with a telescopic sight.

"Martin Luther King, Jr., was a truly brave man," testified Ralph Abernathy. "Had he been a coward rather than a truly brave man, then none of the rest of us would have followed him and we might still be riding in the back of buses and eating in segregated restaurants."

Courage faces fear and thereby masters it. Cowardice represses fear and is thereby mastered by it. Courageous men never lose the zest for living even though their life situation is zestless; cowardly men, overwhelmed by the uncertainties of life, lose the will to live. We must constantly build dykes of courage to hold back the flood of fear.

—*The Strength to Love*, p. 111

Thucydides, that eminent student of the human saga, touched upon lasting truth in his funeral speech for Pericles when he said, "The secret of happiness is freedom, and secret of freedom, courage."

—"Montgomery Sparked a Revolution," *The Southern Courier*, December 11, 1965
(see FEAR)

CRIMINAL

"The most dangerous criminal may be the man gifted with reason, but with no morals." King wrote these words at the age of nineteen in his first published article, titled "The Pursuit of Education," during his senior year at Morehouse College. The daring and dramatic flair that would soon catapult him to public prominence showed itself when he cited as an example of such a "criminal" former Georgia governor Eugene Talmadge. The governor, wrote King, had a Phi Betta Kappa key and "one of the better minds of Georgia, or even America ... yet he contends that I am an inferior being."

CRISIS

"Constructive crisis" was a goal of King's mass demonstrations, peace marches, freedom walks, and civil disobedience tactics. When he was accused of creating tensions, he replied that the tensions were already there; he was merely bringing them to the surface, forcing society to deal with the issues of racism and poverty instead of denying them.

"We set out to precipitate a crisis situation that must open the door to negotiation," he said in a *Playboy* interview. "I am not afraid of the words 'crisis' and 'tension.' I deeply oppose violence, but constructive crisis and tension are necessary for growth."

(see EXPOSURE, TENSION)

CRITICISM

If I sought to answer all of the criticisms that cross my desk, my secretaries would be engaged in little else.

—Letter from Birmingham Jail, 1963

Most of us have an amazing capacity for *external* criticism. We can always see the evil in others. We can always see the evil in our oppressors.

—Sermon, March 22, 1959
(see SELF-CRITICISM)

53

A long line of book buyers waited for Dr. King to autograph their copies of his new book, *Stride Toward Freedom*. It was in Blumstein's department store in Harlem on September 20, 1958. King was seated on a stool behind a table stacked with books, goodnaturedly writing inscriptions on them. A bespectacled black woman named Isola Curry, 42 years old, maneuvered her way to the front of the line.

"Are you Dr. King?" she asked.

"Yes, I am."

"Luther King, I been after you for five years."

Steel flashed as she pulled a sharp Japanese letter opener from her shirt and plunged it into King's chest. He gasped and collapsed.

There was scrambling and confusion. Someone grabbed Mrs. Curry, who was raving dementedly. Another man tried to pull out the letter opener, which was protruding from King's chest. But King stopped him wordlessly, shaking his head. He was taken to the nearest hospital. The letter opener was still sticking out of his chest as he was wheeled into the operating room.

King was operated on by a black surgeon, Dr. Aubrey Maynard, who removed the letter opener, assisted by three others. Maynard made a cross-shaped incision in King's chest. By the time King recovered consciousness some hours later, Coretta was at his side. When Dr. Maynard looked in later and found his patient awake, he offered a strange compliment.

"It's a good thing you were so calm about the whole thing, Dr. King," he said. "The point of the blade was touching your aorta. If you'd moved suddenly, if you'd so much as sneezed, you would have died instantly. You'd have drowned in your own blood."

King said he was grateful to God to be alive.

"We had to remove two ribs," explained Dr. Maynard,

"in order to get the letter opener free, but we've done everything possible. Complications could set in, so we can't be sure for three days, but we're confident your recovery will be complete."

King nodded slowly, touching gently the bandages on his chest.

"You may be interested to know," added the doctor, "I made the incision over your heart in the form of a cross. Since the scar will be there permanently, and you're a minister, it seemed somehow appropriate."

(see Biography 1958, SNEEZE)

CUSTOMS

During a meeting with white leaders of Montgomery during the boycott in 1956, members of the White Citizens Council raised many objections to changing the "cherished customs" of segregation. Dr. King stood up and answered these objections. "It has been argued that any change in present conditions would mean going against 'cherished customs' of our community. But if the customs are wrong we have every reason in the world to change them.

"The decision which we must make now is whether we will give our allegiance to outmoded and unjust customs or to the ethical demands of the universe. As Christians we owe our ultimate allegiance to God and His will, rather than to man and his folkways."

(see MONTGOMERY, SEGREGATION)

D

DEATH

"No man is free if he fears death," King told a Birmingham crowd at a rally on May 3, 1963. "But the minute you conquer the fear of death, at that moment, you are free."

King was often warned of assassination threats against him. He had a standard reply. "If you are cut down in a movement that is designed to save the soul of a nation," he would say, "then no other death could be more redemptive."

When people urged him to take fewer risks, he shrugged them off. "I cannot worry about my safety," he explained. "I cannot live in fear. I have to function. If there is one fear I have conquered it is the fear of death."

I submit to you that if a man hasn't discovered something that he will die for, he isn't fit to live!

—Speech, Cobo Hall, Detroit, June 23, 1963

Death is inevitable.... We need not fear it. The God who brought our whirling planet from primal vapor and has led the human pilgrimage for lo these many centuries can most assuredly lead us through death's dark night into the bright daybreak of eternal life.

—*The Strength to Love*, p. 116

Our earthly life is a prelude to a glorious new awakening, and death is an open door that leads us into eternal life.

—*The Strength to Love*, p. 86
(see GOD, HEAVEN)

DEFEAT

Our consolation is that no one can know the true taste of victory if he has never swallowed defeat.

—*Where Do We Go from Here?* p. 138
(see VICTORY)

DEMOCRACY

King never lost faith in democracy. Even after he was found guilty of trumped-up charges and fined in a Montgomery court for leading the bus boycott on March 22, 1956, he urged his fellow protesters to keep their faith in the democratic system.

"Let us not lose faith in democracy," he said. "For with all of its weaknesses, there is a ground and a basis of hope in our democratic creed."

The democratic ideal of freedom and equality will be fulfilled for all—or all human beings will share in the resulting social and spiritual doom.

—*Stride Toward Freedom*, p. 196
(see AMERICAN DEMOCRACY, DREAM,
FREEDOM, WORLD REVOLUTION)

DEMONSTRATIONS

White Americans must be made to understand the basic motives underlying Negro demonstrations. Many pent-up resentments and latent frustrations are boiling inside the Negro, and he must release them. It is not a threat but a fact of history that if an oppressed people's pent-up emotions are not nonviolently released, they will be violently released.

—Letter from Birmingham Jail, 1963

In the past our demonstrations ... have been highly successful precisely because they were unique in doing three things: first, they called attention to the evil; second, they aroused the conscience of the community; third, they eliminated the evil *itself* when men, women and children stood firm and accepted what came.

—President's annual report to SCLC convention, October 1, 1964
(see CIVIL DISOBEDIENCE)

DESEGREGATION

"I have the feeling that within the next ten years desegregation will be a reality all over the South," declared Dr. King in a dinner speech on May 17, 1962. At the time it sounded like an impossible dream, but it proved to be a prophetic statement.

(see INTEGRATION, SEGREGATION)

DIALECTICAL METHOD

As a practical philosopher, Dr. King employed the dialectical method. He generally rejected the "either-or" method of reasoning in favor of the "both-and" approach. For instance, his approach to racial issues was black-and-white, not black-or-white. So was his approach to all philosophical issues. "Life at its best is a creative synthesis of opposites in fruitful harmony," he wrote in the opening paragraph of *The Strength to Love*.

King continually sought the agreement of opposites, the coming together of contraries, the unification beyond all divisions. Black and white, East and West, capitalist and communist, liberal and conservative, poor and rich, developed nations and undeveloped nations, Christian and nonChristian, and so forth—always he sought the common ground, the common brotherhood of both, the place where the twain meet. He believed this was realistic rather than idealistic. "The realistic attitude," he said, "seeks to reconcile the truths of two opposites and avoid the extremes of both."

During the 1950s, when Martin Luther King was rising to prominence, the United States was in the throes of the cold war and the McCarthy era. The McCarthyist attitude toward communism was rigidly either-or, as was the attitude of FBI Director J. Edgar Hoover, who accused King of being a communist. The conflict between J. Edgar Hoover and Martin Luther King is a classic example of the clash between a nondialectical thinker and a dialectical thinker.

(see COMMUNISM, HOOVER, SYNTHESIS)

DIRECT ACTION

The Negro can take direct action against injustice without waiting for the government to act or a majority to agree with him or a court to rule in his favor.

—*Stride Toward Freedom*, p. 211

We will take direct action against injustice without waiting for other agencies to act. We will not obey unjust laws or submit to unjust practices. We will do this peacefully, openly, cheerfully because our aim is to persuade. We will adopt the means of nonviolence because our end is a community at peace with itself.

—Credo of nonviolent direct action, *Stride Toward Freedom*, p. 216

You may well ask: "Why direct action? Why sit-ins, marches and so forth? Isn't negotiation a better path?" You are quite right in calling for negotiation. Indeed, this is the very purpose of direct action. Nonviolent direct action seeks to create such a crisis and foster such a tension that a community which has constantly refused to negotiate is forced to confront the issue. It seeks so to dramatize the issue that it can no longer be ignored.

—Letter from Birmingham Jail, 1963
(see also NONVIOLENCE, NONVIOLENT RESISTANCE)

DISARMAMENT

I do not minimize the complexity of the problems that need to be faced in achieving disarmament and peace. But I am convinced that we shall not have the will, the courage, and the insight to deal with such matters unless in this field we are prepared to undergo a mental and spiritual reevaluation, a change of focus which will enable us to see that the things that seem most real and powerful are indeed now unreal and have come under sentence of death.

—*Where Do We Go From Here?* p. 185
(see ARMS RACE, PEACE, WAR)

DISCONTENT

I have not said to my people: "Get rid of your discontent." Rather, I have tried to say that this normal and healthy discontent can be channeled into the creative outlet of nonviolent direct action.

—Letter from Birmingham Jail, 1963

The deep rumbling of discontent that we hear today is the thunder of disinherited masses, rising from dungeons of oppression to the bright hills of freedom.

—Nobel lecture, December 11, 1964
(see REVOLUTION, WORLD REVOLUTION)

DIVISION

King encountered fierce heckling during a mass rally at Chicago's Liberty Baptist Church on August 31, 1966. As he described the Chicago settlement he was continually interrupted by booing and shouts of "Black Power!"

Unable to proceed, King asked if there was someone who wanted to speak. The President of the Chicago chapter of the Student Nonviolent Coordinating Committee, which had become a rival organization to King's Southern Christian Leadership Conference in the freedom movement, came to the podium and delivered a scathing attack on the Chicago agreement and against King himself.

Returning to the microphone, King shook his head and said: "Whenever Pharaoh wanted to keep the slaves in slavery, he kept them fighting among themselves." This remark struck a responsive cord with the crowd. The hecklers fell silent.

(see UNITY)

DOG BITES

It was front-page news across the country when police dogs were released by Commissioner Eugene "Bull" Connor to attack nonviolent demonstrators in Birmingham in the spring of 1963. One photograph of a dog closing its jaws on a black child was published nationally and seen by President Kennedy, who said it made him "sick."

Dr. King urged the protesters not to be afraid of the dogs.

"Well, I'll tell you," he said at a Birmingham rally. "When I was growing up, I was dog bitten—For *nothing*! So I don't mind being bitten by a dog for standing up for freedom!"

(see CHILDREN, FREEDOM)

DREAM

Again and again King spoke of The Dream. It was a dream "deeply rooted in the American Dream." But it was not limited to America. It encompassed all of humanity. It was a dream of the Beloved Community.

The Dream was Martin Luther King's vision of a Promised Land. The Dream originated in the mind of God, he believed. He saw himself as a channel for the communication of God's dream to God's people. He saw himself as following in the footsteps of Amos, Micah, and Isaiah, whose teachings were inspired by a Biblical God.

King described this dream many times in many forms before arriving at his most famous formulation expressed in his celebrated speech on the steps of the Lincoln Memorial in 1963.

"The dream is one of equality of opportunity, of privilege and property widely distributed," he wrote in a 1960 article published in *YWCA Magazine*, "a dream of a land where men will not take necessities from the many to give luxuries to the few; a dream of a land where men do not argue that the color of a man's skin determines the content of his character; a dream of a place where all our gifts and resources are held not for ourselves alone but as instruments of service for the rest of humanity; the dream of a country where every man will respect the dignity and worth of all human personality, and men will dare to live together as brothers. . . . Whenever it is fulfilled, we will emerge from the bleak and desolate midnight of man's inhumanity to man into the bright and glowing daybreak of freedom and justice for all of God's children."

In a speech in Detroit's Cobo Hall on June 23, 1963, King used the line "I have a dream" and the crowd roared in response. He remembered this refrain two months later and used it again.

At the conclusion of the March on Washington on August 28, 1963, King addressed a crowd of approximately 250,000. It was the most carefully written address he had ever delivered. He had worked on it most of the preceding two days and stayed up all the previous night.

The last speaker of a long afternoon of oratory, King was introduced by Asa Randolph as "the moral leader of our nation." The crowd burst into applause and the band struck up "Battle Hymn of the Republic."

Standing with the Lincoln Memorial behind him, Dr. King delivered what may go down in history as the greatest American speech since Lincoln's Gettysburg address. The parallel was not coincidental. "He intended to echo some of the Lincolnian language," Coretta recalled.

Several minutes into the speech, King decided to abandon his text. Mahalia Jackson, who was seated behind him, shouted out: "Tell them about the dream!" It is not known whether he heard her, but he decided to tell the crowd—and the nation that was watching on television—about the dream.

I say to you today, my friends, that even though we face the difficulties of today and tomorrow, I still have a dream. It is a dream deeply rooted in the American dream.

I have a dream that one day this nation will rise up and live out the true meaning of its creed: "We hold these truths to be self-evident; that all men are created equal."

I have a dream that one day, on the red hills of Georgia, sons of former slaves and the sons of former slaveowners will be able to sit down together at the table of brotherhood.

I have a dream that my four little children will one day live in a nation where they will not be judged by the color of their skin but by the content of their character.

I have a dream today.

I have a dream that one day, down in Alabama, with its vicious racists, with its governor having his lips dripping with the words of interposition and nullification, one day right there in Alabama, little black boys and black girls will be able to join hands with little white boys and white girls and walk together as sisters and brothers.

I have a dream today.

I have a dream that one day "every valley shall be exalted, every hill and mountain shall be made low, the rough places will be made plains, and the crooked places will be made straight, and the glory of the Lord shall be revealed, and all flesh shall see it together."

This is our hope. This is the faith that I go back to the South with. With this faith we will be able to hew out of the mountain of despair a stone of hope. With this faith we will be able to transform the jangling discords of our nation into a beautiful symphony of brotherhood. With this faith we will be able to work together, to pray together, to struggle together, to stand up for freedom together, knowing that we will be free one day.

And this will be the day. This will be the day when all of God's children will be able to sing with new meaning, "My country 'tis of thee, sweet land of liberty, of thee I sing. Land where my fathers died, land of the pilgrim's pride, from every mountainside, let freedom ring."

And if America is to be a great nation this must become true. So let freedom ring from the prodigious hilltops of New Hampshire. Let freedom ring from the mighty mountains of New York. Let freedom ring from the heightening Alleghenies of Pennsylvania!

Let freedom ring from the snowcapped Rockies of Colorado!

Let freedom ring from the curvaceous slopes of California!

But not only that; let freedom ring from Stone Mountain

of Georgia! Let freedom ring from Lookout Mountain of Tennessee.

Let freedom ring from every hill and molehill of Mississippi. From every mountainside, let freedom ring.

And when this happens, and when we allow freedom to ring, when we let it ring from every village and every hamlet, from every state and every city, we will be able to speed up that day when all of God's children, black men and white men, Jews and Gentiles, Protestants and Catholics, will be able to join hands and sing in the words of that old Negro spiritual, "Free at last! Free at last! Thank God almighty, we are free at last!"

Immediately after the speech, King and the principal leaders of the March were invited to meet with President Kennedy at the White House. As they filed into the Cabinet room, a smiling President Kennedy greeted King with the words, "I have a dream."

(see AMERICAN DREAM)

DUALISM

"Each of us is something of a schizophrenic personality. We're split up and divided against ourselves," asserted King in his sermon "Loving Your Enemies." "There is something of a civil war going on within all our lives." He spoke from personal experience.

When fame came to King, his public role took so much of his attention that it left him little time and little opportunity to be himself. He became a symbol of something much larger than himself—the civil rights movement—and this made him appear larger than life to others. Like other famous men before him, he became conscious of a duality in his life.

"He couldn't understand his career," recollected J. Pius Barbour, one of his closest colleagues. "All the publicity he'd gotten as a civil rights leader.... He said, 'There's a kind of dualism in my life.' . . . He always said that Martin Luther King the famous man was a kind of stranger to him."

Barbour remembers being with Dr. King in his study at home one afternoon when King stood before the full-length mirror and shook his head and confessed, "Doc, I am conscious of two Martin Luther Kings. I'm a wonder to myself!"

(see HIGHER SELF, SINNER)

DU BOIS, W.E.B.

"He confronted the establishment as a model of militant manhood and integrity," said King in a tribute to the black writer W.E.B. Du Bois at Carnegie Hall on February 28, 1968. "He defied them and though they heaped venom and scorn on him, his powerful voice was never stilled."

King admired the author of *The Souls of Black Folk* but did not feel that Du Bois had the answer for American blacks. He saw Du Bois as a black aristocrat, and aristocracies—black or white—were primarily concerned with saving themselves, not the whole people. "Yet, in the very nature of Du Bois' outlook there was not room for the whole people," King wrote in *Why We Can't Wait*. "It was a tactic for an aristocratic elite who would themselves be benefited while leaving behind the 'untalented' ninety percent."

E

ECONOMIC INJUSTICE

The inseparable twin of racial injustice is economic injustice.

—The Strength to Love, p. 137

Many white Americans of good will have never connected bigotry with economic exploitation. They have deplored prejudice but tolerated or ignored economic injustice. But the Negro knows these two evils have a malignant kinship.

—Why We Can't Wait, p. 24

Since emancipation the Negro American has continued to suffer under an essentially unreconstructed economy. He was freed without land or legal protection, and was made an outcast entitled only to the most menial jobs. Even the federal government that set him free failed to work out any long-range policy that would guarantee economic resources to a previously enslaved people.

—Stride Toward Freedom, p. 202

It is impossible to create a formula for the future which does not take into account that our society has been doing something special *against* the Negro for hundreds of years. How then can he be absorbed into the mainstream of American life if we do not do something special *for* him now, in order to balance the equation and equip him to compete on an equal basis?

—*Why We Can't Wait*, p. 134

Negroes are still at the bottom of the economic ladder. They live within two concentric circles of segregation. One imprisons them on the basis of color, while the other confines them within a separate culture of poverty.

—*Why We Can't Wait*, p. 23

He is deprived of normal education and normal social and economic opportunities. When he seeks opportunity, he is told, in effect, to lift himself up by his own bootstraps, advice which does not take into account the fact that he is barefoot.

—*Why We Can't Wait*, p. 23

The Negroes' problem cannot be solved unless the whole of American society takes a new turn toward greater economic justice.

—*Where Do We Go from Here?* p. 50
(see BILL OF RIGHTS FOR THE DISADVANTAGED, ECONOMIC REFORM, POVERTY)

ECONOMIC REFORM

After religious and civil liberties are secured, the next frontier of freedom is economic freedom. Liberation is not complete until freedom from poverty and economic exploitation is achieved.

"What will it profit him to be able to send his children

to an integrated school if the family income is insufficient to buy them school clothes?" asked King. "What will he gain by being permitted to move to an integrated neighborhood if he cannot afford to do so because he is unemployed or has a low-paying job with no future?"

In his final years of life, King shifted the focus of his attention from civil rights to economic rights. At the time of his death he was expanding his movement to include all economically deprived people of all races and creeds, in America and abroad. He called it the Poor People's Campaign. Two of the measures he proposed were a Bill of Rights for the Disadvantaged and a Guaranteed National Income.

New laws are not enough. The emergency we now face is economic, and it is a desperately worsening situation.

—*The Trumpet of Conscience*, p. 55

One point in the Negro's program should be a plan to improve his own economic lot. Through the establishment of credit unions, savings and loan associations, and cooperative enterprises the Negro can greatly improve his economic status. He must develop habits of thrift and techniques of wise investment. He must not wait for the end of segregation that lies at the basis of his economic deprivation; he must act now to lift himself up.

—*Stride Toward Freedom*, p. 222
(see BILL OF RIGHTS FOR THE DISADVANTAGED, GUARANTEED NATIONAL INCOME, POVERTY)

EDUCATION

Dr. King received the best education available in his time. His Crozer Seminary degree was sufficient qualification for his role as a reverend pastor, but he went on to obtain a doctorate degree from Boston University as well. He was one of the best educated individuals in America, black or white. He always felt that it was his education, more than anything else, that prepared him for his leadership role.

King believed education was the path out of poverty and racism and the key to social awareness and activism. If education is the answer, the question is *how*. "How shall we turn the ghettos into a vast school?" asked King. "How shall we make every street corner a forum, not a lounging place for trivial gossip and petty gambling, where life is wasted and human experience withers to trivial sensations? How shall we make every houseworker and every laborer a demonstrator, a voter, a canvasser and a student?"

Education is more than ever the passport to decent economic positions.

—*Where Do We Go from Here?* p. 193

The task is considerable; it is not merely to bring Negroes up to higher educational levels, but to close the gap between their educational levels and those of whites. If this does not happen, as the Negroes advance educationally, whites will be moving ahead even more rapidly.

—*Where Do We Go from Here?* p. 194

Parents should be involved in the schools to a much greater extent, breaking down the barriers between professionals and the community they serve.

—*Where Do We Go from Here?* p. 194

Education without social action is a one-sided value because it has no true power potential. Social action without education is a weak expression of pure energy. Deeds uninformed by educated thought can take false directions.

When we go into action and confront our adversaries, we
must be as armed with knowledge as they.

—*Where Do We Go from Here?* p. 155

Quality education for all is most likely to come through
educational parks which bring together in one place all
the students of a large area. Because of the economies of
large-scale operation, the educational park will make practical a multiplicity of teaching specialists and superb facilities.

—*Where Do We Go from Here?* p. 195
(see ENGLISH GRAMMAR, EXCELLENCE, STUDENTS)

EISENHOWER, DWIGHT D.

After the success of the Montgomery Bus Boycott in 1956,
King sent a telegram to President Eisenhower asking the
President to meet with a Negro delegation to discuss civil
rights. President Eisenhower never replied to the telegram.

King continued to persist, however, and eventually a
meeting at the White House occurred on June 23, 1958. At
this meeting Eisenhower endorsed the need for more voting rights legislation, but no substantive action was taken.

Although he admitted that he voted for Eisenhower in
1956, King was not overly impressed by President Eisenhower's performance. He felt that Eisenhower was unwilling to use the power of the presidency to advance the
cause of civil rights.

"I fear that future historians will have to record that
when America came to its most progressive moment of
creative fulfillment in the area of human relations, it was
temporarily held back by a chief executive who refused to
make a strong positive statement morally condemning
segregation."

* * *

President Eisenhower could not be committed to anything which involved a structural change in the architecture of American society. His conservatism was fixed and rigid, and any evil defacing the nation had to be extracted bit by bit with a tweezer because the surgeon's knife was an instrument too radical to touch this best of all possible societies.

—*Why We Can't Wait*, p. 143

EMANCIPATION PROCLAMATION

During a visit to the White House in 1961, President Kennedy took King on a tour of the historic mansion. While they were strolling through the Lincoln Room, King seized the opportunity to make a request. Noting a framed copy of the Emancipation Proclamation on the wall, King said to Kennedy: "Mr. President, I'd like to see you stand in this room and sign a second Emancipation Proclamation outlawing segregation, one hundred years after Lincoln's. You could base it on the Fourteenth Amendment." President Kennedy responded agreeably, suggesting that King prepare such a proclamation for him to consider.

It turned out that no such proclamation was signed. On the anniversary of the Emancipation Proclamation, January 1, 1963, a large reception for prominent blacks was held at the White House. King was invited, but disappointed with Kennedy's reluctance to make a stronger moral statement on the race issue and sign a second Emancipation Proclamation, he declined to attend. Six months later, however, President Kennedy announced his civil rights bill, demonstrating for the first time the type of Presidential leadership on civil rights for which King had been calling.

(see KENNEDY ASSASSINATION)

ENDS

People often separate the ends and the means, claiming the means justify the ends if the ends are good. But Martin Luther King contended that the ends could not be separated from the means. Those who assert that evil means can lead to good ends are deceiving themselves.

"We will never have peace in the world," he said, "until men everywhere recognize that ends are not cut off from means, because the means represent the ideal in the making, and the end in process."

If we are to have peace in the world, men and nations must embrace the nonviolent affirmation that ends and means must cohere.

—*The Trumpet of Conscience*, p. 70

We must pursue peaceful ends through peaceful means.

—*The Trumpet of Conscience*, p. 71
(see MEANS, MORAL RELATIVITY)

ENGLISH GRAMMAR

A firm believer in good grammar and proper English usage, King was particularly critical of professionals who were sloppy in their speech.

"I have met more school teachers recently who wouldn't know a verb if it was as big as that table," he said in a speech on December 5, 1957. "For a college graduate to be standing up talking about 'you is'—there is no excuse for it! And some of these people are teaching our children, and crippling our children!"

(see EDUCATION)

EULOGY

Martin Luther King's mentor at Morehouse College was Dr. Benjamin Mays, a brilliant man and eloquent speaker. Dr. Mays was equally admiring of young Martin Luther King, whose eloquence as an orator was already becoming legendary.

When King returned to his alma mater Morehouse to receive an honorary degree in 1957 after the Montgomery Bus Boycott, Dr. Mays shook his hand and said to him: "I want you to preach my eulogy."

King replied: "I want you to preach mine."

As fate would have it, Dr. Mays did preach the younger man's eulogy on April 9, 1968.

"We have assembled here from every section of this great nation," declared Dr. Mays on that sad occasion, "and from other parts of the world to give thanks to God that He gave to America, at this moment in history, Martin Luther King, Jr.

"Truly God is no respecter of persons. How strange! God called the grandson of a slave to his father's side, and said to him: 'Martin Luther, speak to America about war and peace; about social justice and racial discrimination; about its obligation to the poor; and about nonviolence as a way of perfecting social change in a world of brutality and war.' "

(see FUNERAL)

EVIL

Evil often appears to win. But the apparent triumph of evil is only temporary, according to King. Evil cannot prevail indefinitely against the will of God.

"Evil in the form of injustice and exploitation shall not survive forever," he wrote in *The Strength to Love*. "A Red Sea passage in history ultimately brings the forces of goodness to victory, and the closing of the same waters marks the doom and destruction of the forces of evil. This reminds us that evil carries the seed of its own destruction. . . . It can go a long way, but then it reaches its limit."

The Hitlers and the Mussolinis have their day, and for a period they may wield great power, spreading themselves like a green bay tree, but soon they are cut down like the grass and wither as the green herb.

—The Strength to Love, p. 103

Death is not the ultimate evil; the ultimate evil is to be outside God's love.

—The Strength to Love, p. 91

The chain reaction of evil—hate begetting hate, wars producing more wars—must be broken, or we shall be plunged into the dark abyss of annihilation.

—The Strength to Love, p. 3

Something about evil we must never forget, namely, that evil is recalcitrant and determined, and never voluntarily relinquishes its hold short of a persistent, almost fanatical resistance.

—The Strength to Love, p. 60

Evil is not merely a principle of nonbeing or an absence of something. It is both positive and aggressive.

—King's Ph.D. dissertation, 1955, p. 220

Evil is stark, grim and collossally real.

—The Strength to Love, p. 58

Structures of evil do not crumble by passive waiting. . . . Evil must be attacked by a counteracting persistence, by the day-to-day assault of the battering rams of justice.

—*Where Do We Go from Here?* p. 128

To ignore evil is to become an accomplice to it.

—*Where Do We Go from Here?* p. 86

Noncooperation with evil is as much a moral obligation as is cooperation with good.

—*Stride Toward Freedom*, p. 212

As we struggle to defeat the forces of evil, the God of the universe struggles with us. Evil dies on the seashore, not merely because of man's endless struggle against it, but because of God's power to defeat it.

—*The Strength to Love*, p. 64

The forces of evil may temporarily conquer truth, but truth will ultimately conquer its conquerer.

—*The Strength to Love*, p. 105

I believe that unarmed truth and unconditional love will have the final word and reality. This is why right temporarily defeated is stronger than evil triumphant.

—Nobel address, December 11, 1964
(see also GOD, HISTORY, SIN)

EXCELLENCE

"Now if you have the illusion at any point that our job will be merely to compete with Negroes in this new age that is emerging, you're sleeping through a revolution," said Dr. King to an audience of black businessmen in Chicago on August 24, 1963. "We must set out to do our jobs

76

so well that the living, the dead, or the unborn couldn't do them any better."

Even though slavery and segregation were designed to make the Negro adjust patiently to mediocrity, we must work assiduously to aspire to excellence.

—*Where Do We Go from Here?* p. 126
(see ACHIEVEMENT, EDUCATION)

EXPOSURE

The first step in eliminating injustice is exposing it, according to King. Exposing racism, inequity, violence, and evil to the light—this is King's method for initiating reform. King felt that racism and hatred were cancers eating away at the heart of American democracy.

"We did not cause the cancer; we merely exposed it," he wrote in *Where Do We Go from Here: Chaos or Community?* "Only through this kind of exposure will the cancer ever be cured."

(see CRISIS, MASS MEDIA, TENSION)

EXTREMISM

Was not Jesus an extremist for love: "Love your enemies, bless them that curse you, do good to them that hate you, and pray for them which despitefully use you, and persecute you." Was not Amos an extremist for justice: "Let justice roll down like waters and righteousness like an ever-flowing stream." Was not Paul an extremist for the Christian gospel: "I bear in my body the marks of the Lord Jesus." Was not Martin Luther an extremist: "Here I stand; I cannot do otherwise, so help me God." And John Bunyan: "I will stay in jail to the end of my days before I make a butchery of my conscience." And Abraham Lincoln: "This nation cannot survive half slave and half free."

And Thomas Jefferson: "We hold these truths to be self-evident, that all men are created equal . . ." So the question is not whether we will be extremists, but what kind of extremists we will be. Will we be extremists for hate or for love? Will we be extremists for the preservation of injustice or for the extension of justice?

—Letter from Birmingham Jail, 1963
(see LEADER, NONCONFORMISM, REVOLUTION)

FAMILY

Nothing is so much needed as a secure family life for a people seeking to rise out of poverty and backwardness.

—*Where Do We Go from Here?* p. 106
(see BLACK FAMILY, GHETTO)

FATALISM

Because freedom is a part of the essence of man, the fatalist, by denying freedom, becomes a puppet, not a person.

—*The Strength to Love,* p. 81
(see FREEDOM)

FBI

The hostility of FBI director J. Edgar Hoover toward Martin Luther King commenced shortly after the Kennedy inauguration, when King published an article in *Nation* magazine that made a parenthetical reference to the Federal Bureau of Investigation:

79

"If, for instance, the law-enforcement personnel in the FBI were integrated, many persons who now defy federal law might come under restraints from which they are presently free."

This appeared to be a criticism of the FBI, and Hoover responded with wrath to any criticism of his beloved bureau. King was publicly declared to be "in error" in alleging that the FBI was segregated. Hoover's view was that if even *one* black man was employed by the agency, the agency was not segregated.

The controversy over the segregation of the FBI was just beginning. Attorney General Robert Kennedy ordered that the FBI be integrated immediately, but Hoover resisted the order, using the same logic, namely, that the FBI was already integrated. One day Robert Kennedy, who was Hoover's immediate superior, stormed into Hoover's office and demanded to know how many black agents were employed by the FBI. "Five," was Hoover's reply. But Hoover did not point out that all five were employed by him as personal servants, including his chauffer.

(see HOOVER)

FEAR

The day after his court conviction for leading the Montgomery Bus Boycott, King held a press conference and told reporters he would not allow himself to be intimidated, he would not succumb to fear.

"An individual must stand up and be counted and be willing to face the consequences, whatever they are. If he is filled with fear, he cannot do it. And my great prayer is always that God will save me from the paralysis of crippling fear, because I think when a person lives with the fear of the consequences for his personal life, he can never do anything in terms of lifting the whole of humanity and solving many of the social problems that we confront."

In one of his favorite sermons, "Antidotes to Fear," King preached that wars are caused by fear rather than hate; that racial conflict is rooted in fear rather than hate. Racial discrimination against blacks in America was caused by white people's fears of blacks.

How does one overcome fear? First, "we must unflinchingly face our fears." Then we master fear by developing three of the greatest virtues in human nature: courage, love, and faith.

"We can master fear through one of the supreme virtues known to man—courage," he said. "Courage is the power of the mind to overcome fear . . .

"Courage faces fear and thereby masters it. Cowardice represses fear and is thereby mastered by it . . .

"Fear is mastered by love . . . such love confronts evil without flinching.

"Fear is mastered by faith." Faith in God can overcome all fears. Faith does not exempt us from pain and struggle. "Rather, it instills us with the inner equilibrium needed to face strains, burdens, and fears that inevitably come, and assures us that the universe is trustworthy and that God is concerned."

Our problem is not to be rid of fear but rather to harness and master it.

—The Strength to Love, p. 110

Is not fear one of the major causes of war? We say that war is a consequence of hate, but close scrutiny reveals this sequence: first fear, then hate, then war, and finally deeper hatred.

—The Strength to Love, p. 112

Love casts out fear.

—*The Strength to Love*, p. 112
(see COURAGE, HATRED, LOVE)

FIRST DATE

Martin Luther King proposed to Coretta Scott on their first date. It was a lunch date at Sharaf's Restaurant on Massachusetts Avenue in Boston, where they ate a cafeteria-style meal between her twelve and one o'clock Conservatory classes.

He was impressed by her conversational abilities. "Oh, I see you know about some other things besides music," he said enthusiastically, and launched into a wide-ranging discussion of politics, philosophy, art, religion, and history.

She was not as impressed by him as he was by her. "My first thought was 'How short he seems,' and the second was, 'How unimpressive he looks.' Her initial overall impression of him was of "an older man, pious, narrow-minded, and not too well-trained."

Within a few minutes, however, she changed her mind. "When he talked, he grew in stature," she observed. "He radiated charm." She soon found herself entranced. But when he brought up the subject of marriage at the end of their date, she put him off.

Sitting in the car before dropping her off at the conservatory, he said: "You have everything I ever wanted in a wife. There are only four things, and you have them all."

"I don't see how you can say that," she replied, taken by surprise. "You don't even know me."

"I can tell," he said. "The four things I look for in a wife are character, intelligence, personality, and beauty. And you have them all. When can I see you again?"

She kept calm. "I'll have to check my schedule," she said with a smile. "You may call me later."

He did. Soon they were engaged.

(see Biography 1953, HONEYMOON, WEDDING)

FORGIVENESS

Forgiveness is not an occasional act; it is a permanent attitude.

—*The Strength to Love*, p. 26

We must develop and maintain the capacity to forgive. He who is devoid of the power to forgive is devoid of the power of love.

—*The Strength to Love*, p. 35

The degree to which we are able to forgive determines the degree to which we are able to love our enemies.

—*The Strength to Love*, p. 35
(see CHRISTIAN LOVE, HATRED, LOVE)

FREEDOM

King liked to tell this story of a young freedom marcher in Birmingham.

"A child of no more than eight walked with her mother one day in a demonstration. An amused policeman leaned down to her and said with mock gruffness, 'What do you want?'

"The child looked into his eyes, unafraid, and gave her answer.

" 'F'eedom,' she said.

"She could not even pronounce the word," he wrote later in *Why We Can't Wait*, "but no Gabriel trumpet could have sounded a truer note."

* * *

It is no more possible to be half free than it is to be half alive.

—*Why We Can't Wait*, p. 128

We do not want freedom fed to us in teaspoons over another 150 years.

—King statement, Miami, February 12, 1958

Freedom is never voluntarily given by the oppressor; it must be demanded by the oppressed.

—Letter from Birmingham Jail, 1963

We will be sadly mistaken if we think freedom is some lavish dish that the federal government and the white man will pass out on a silver platter while the Negro merely furnishes the appetite.

—Quoted in "King Tells Goals,"
Chicago Tribune, July 11, 1966, p. 2

If the inexpressible cruelties of slavery could not stop us, the opposition we now face will surely fail. We will win our freedom because the sacred heritage of our nation and the eternal will of God are embodied in our echoing demands.

—Letter from Birmingham Jail, 1963

Freedom is not won by a passive acceptance of suffering. Freedom is won by a struggle *against* suffering.

—*Where Do We Go from Here?* p. 20

We are both free and destined. Freedom is the act of deliberating, deciding, and responding within our destined nature.

—*The Strength to Love*, p. 81

Freedom is necessary for one's selfhood, for one's intrinsic worth.

—Speech, Durham, North Carolina, February 16, 1959

We will reach the goal of freedom in Birmingham and all over the nation, because the goal of America is freedom.

—Letter from Birmingham Jail, 1963

The essence of man is found in freedom.

—*Where Do We Go from Here?* p. 98
(see AMERICA, CHOICE, DREAM, MAN)

FREEDOM FIGHTER

The Freedom Movement was served by thousands of volunteers who received neither publicity nor salary. One of the few paid staff members during the Birmingham campaign was James Orange, nicknamed Sunshine. When the Birmingham campaign was over, it was necessary to terminate the paid staff, including James Orange. A week later, Orange showed up at the SCLC headquarters in Atlanta and asked to see King and Abernathy.

"I just want to say something about your letter terminating my service," said Orange. "When you all came to town I quit the steel mills and joined with the Movement. It was the greatest thing that ever happened in my life. I want you to know you didn't hire me and you can't fire me. I will be with the Movement till they say 'Ashes to ashes, dust to dust' over me. I'm a Freedom Fighter and I'll die a Freedom Fighter."

Abernathy cleared his throat. "But the money ... Sunshine, we just don't—"

"If you have the money, I know you'll pay me. If you don't, that's okay, too. But I'm still a Freedom Fighter. Understand?"

"In that case," said King, grinning, "you're still on the staff."

FREEDOM MOVEMENT

The Negro freedom movement would have been historic and worthy even if it had only served the cause of civil rights. But its laurels are greater because it stimulated a broader social movement that elevated the moral level of the nation. In the struggle against the evils of the society, decent values were preserved. Moreover, a significant body of young people learned that in opposing the tyrannical forces that were crushing them they added stature and meaning to their lives.

—*The Trumpet of Conscience*, p. 47

What we are seeing now is a freedom explosion.

—Nobel address, December 11, 1964

All over the world, like a fever, the freedom movement is spreading in the widest liberation in history. The great masses of people are determined to end the exploitation of their races and land. They are awake and moving toward their goal like a tidal wave. You can hear them rumbling in every village, street, on the docks, in the houses, among the students in the churches and at political meetings.

—Nobel address, December 11, 1964

FREEDOM NOW

Freedom Now! was a King rally cry. He sometimes ended his speeches by chanting it with the crowd.

"What do we want?" he called out.

"Freedom Now!" the crowd responded.

One time during the Selma campaign his son Marty sat

86

behind him on the platform. King turned around and looked at his son.

"Marty ... Marty! What do we want?"

"Freedom!" Marty answered back.

"Marty, when do we want it?"

Marty spoke up: "We want freedom now!"

Freedom Now! might have been a civil rights mantra, but freedom did not come instantaneously; its realization was often a slow and painful process.

"Morally, we ought to have what we say in the slogan, Freedom Now," said King during the Chicago Freedom Campaign of 1966. "But it all doesn't come now. That's a sad fact of life you have to live with."

FREEDOM RIDERS

"It will be a long time before we forget the Freedom Rides. We just decided to take a ride for freedom. And as a result of this we were able to end segregation in interstate travel."

This is Dr. King's brief summary of an episode in the civil rights struggle that preoccupied him and the Kennedy administration throughout the spring and summer of 1961. As the Freedom Riders made their way through Alabama, testing federal desegregation policy in violation of local segregation laws and customs, they encountered tremendous resistance. Local authorities arrested the riders or stood by and watched as they were beaten by vigilantes.

Alabama Governor John Patterson appeared on television and denounced the Freedom Riders and King. "Now, the best thing for King to do is to get out of Alabama as quickly as he can because he's a menace to the peace of this city."

When the Freedom Riders were jailed in Jackson, Mississippi, King received an offer of intervention from Attorney General Robert Kennedy to release the Freedom Riders on bail. King declined RFK's offer. The ensuing phone conversation between the two of them, recalled by themselves and others later, illustrates the issues of civil disobedience and the conflicts between means and ends.

"No, they will stay," said Martin firmly. "It is part of the philosophy of this movement. Our goal is to fill the jails until these evil laws can no longer be used against us."

"This is not a philosophical issue, Martin. What's the charge? Using segregated restrooms? The whole thing is ludicrous! And frankly, it's an embarrassment to the President, who's going to see Kruschev in Vienna next month. This weakens his position. It makes us look ridiculous in the eyes of the world."

"It's a matter of conscience and morality," Martin replied. "These young people have pledged to use their lives and their bodies to right a wrong. Our conscience tells us that the law is wrong and we must resist. But we have a moral obligation to accept the penalty."

Robert Kennedy, like his older brother, was impatient with moralizing. "Where did you get that idea from? Gandhi?"

"Jesus furnished the spirit. Gandhi showed us how it would work. We will capture the conscience of the nation."

"That is not going to have the slightest effect on what the government is going to do. The fact that they stay in jail is not going to have the slightest effect."

The tension between the two men mounted. They were never quite sure whether they were friends, adversaries, friendly adversaries, or adversarial friends.

"Perhaps it would help if students came down here by the hundreds—by the hundreds of thousands," said Martin.

Robert Kennedy stiffened. He spoke sharply.

"This country belongs to you as much as to me. You can determine what's best as well as I can. But don't make statements that sound like threats, Martin. That's not the way to deal with us."

Martin sighed, adopting a more conciliatory tone.

"It's difficult for most men to understand the position of oppressed people. Ours is a way out—it's creative, moral, and nonviolent. It is not tied to black supremacy or communism, but to the plight of the oppressed. It can save the soul of America, Bobby. You must understand that we've made no gains without pressure. And I hope that pressure will always be moral, legal, and peaceful."

"But the problem won't be settled in Jackson. The problem can only be solved by strong federal action. We should be working together, Martin, not against each other."

"Bob, I'm deeply appreciative of what the Administration is doing. I see a ray of hope, but I am different than my father. I feel the need of being free now!"

Robert Kennedy was silent a few moments. "Well, it all depends on what you and the people in jail decide. If they want to get out, we can get them out."

Martin Luther King replied, "They'll stay."

(see CIVIL DISOBEDIENCE, LAW)

FUNERAL

At Martin Luther King's funeral, at the request of Coretta King, a tape recording of the slain leader's voice was played for the assembly of mourners. It was a recording of a prophetic sermon delivered two months earlier, on February 4, 1968, in which King left instructions for his funeral.

"If any of you are around when I have to meet my day, I don't want a long funeral. And if you get somebody to deliver the eulogy, tell him not to talk too long. . . .

"Tell them not to mention that I have a Nobel Peace Prize; that isn't important. Tell them not to mention that I have three or four hundred other awards; that's not important. Tell them not to mention where I went to school.

"I'd like somebody to mention that day that Martin Luther King, Jr., tried to give his life serving others.

"I'd like for somebody to say that day that Martin Luther King, Jr., tried to love somebody. . . .

"I want you to be able to say that day that I did try to feed the hungry. I want you to be able to say that day that I did try in my life to clothe those who were naked. I want you to say on that day that I did try in my life to visit those who were in prison. And I want you to say that I tried to love and serve humanity.

"Yes, if you want to say that I was a drum major, say that I was a drum major for justice; say that I was a drum major for peace; I was a drum major for righteousness. And all the other shallow things will not matter.

"And that's all I want to say . . . if I can help somebody as I pass along. . . . If I can do my duty as a Christian ought, if I can bring salvation to a world once wrought, if I can spread the message as the master taught, then my living will not be in vain."

Martin Luther King had requested a brief, simple service. Instead, his funeral was one of the most conspicuous of the twentieth century. Among the many dignitaries and celebrities attending the funeral were Vice President Hubert Humphrey, Richard Nixon, Stevie Wonder, Attorney General Ramsey Clark, Senator Robert Kennedy, Senator Eugene McCarthy, New York Mayor John Lindsay, Mrs. John F. Kennedy, Marlon Brando, Nelson Rockefeller, fifty members of the House of Representatives, thirty senators, and a host of foreign dignitaries. Some were outraged that President Johnson did not attend, but the President blamed it on the Secret Service, which had warned him the trip to the funeral would be too dangerous to risk.

(see COMMITMENT, EULOGY, JOHNSON)

G

GANDHI

"It is ironic, yet inescapably true that the greatest Christian of the modern world was a man who never embraced Christianity," wrote King in rebuttal to *Christian Century*, a church magazine that had attacked the Gandhi society, saying that its name was un-Christian. "I believe that in some marvelous way, God worked through Gandhi, and the spirit of Jesus Christ saturated his life," replied King, urging a more ecumenical appreciation of God's word.

The greatest single influence on Martin Luther King, other than the gospel of Jesus Christ, was the nonviolent philosophy of Mohandas Gandhi, who led the people of India to independence from Great Britain through the use of nonviolent resistance.

King was introduced to Gandhi's philosophy in 1948 while a student at Crozer Seminary. He immediately saw that Gandhi offered a *method* by which Christ's doctrine of Christian love could be applied to the problems of people struggling to achieve justice and freedom.

"As I delved deeper into the philosophy of Gandhi, my

skepticism concerning the power of love gradually diminished, and I came to see for the first time that the Christian doctrine of love, operating through the Gandhian method of nonviolence, is one of the most potent weapons available to an oppressed people in their struggle for freedom."

In his book *Nonviolent Resistance*, Gandhi expressed the idea of love as a transforming power. "The force of love is the same as the force of soul or truth," wrote Gandhi. "Complete nonviolence is absence of ill will against all that lives. It is pure love."

The power of love was so great that, according to Gandhi, "If one man could achieve the perfect love it is enough to neutralize the hatred of millions."

Gandhi was probably the first person in history to lift the love ethic of Jesus above mere interaction between individuals to a powerful and effective social force on a large scale. . . .

It was in this Gandhian emphasis on love and nonviolence that I discovered the method for social reform that I had been seeking. . . .

I came to feel that this was the only morally and practically sound method open to oppressed people in their struggle for freedom.

—*Stride Toward Freedom*, p. 97

Christ furnished the spirit and motivation, while Gandhi furnished the method.

—*Stride Toward Freedom*, p. 85

Mahatma Gandhi never had more than one hundred persons absolutely committed to his philosophy. But with this small group of devoted followers, he galvanized the whole of India, and through a magnificent feat of nonviolence challenged the might of the British empire and won freedom for his people.

—Stride Toward Freedom, p. 218

My study of Gandhi convinced me that true pacifism is not nonresistance to evil, but nonviolent resistance to evil.

—Stride Toward Freedom, p. 98

Gandhi resisted evil with as much vigor and power as the violent resister, but he resisted with love instead of hate.

—Stride Toward Freedom, p. 98

(see CHRISTIAN LOVE, NONCOOPERATION, NONVIOLENCE)

GARVEY, MARCUS

After the First World War, Marcus Garvey ... called for a return to Africa and a resurgence of race pride.... There was reason to be proud of their heritage as well as their bitterly won achievements in America. Yet his plan was doomed because an exodus to Africa in the twentieth century by a people who had struck roots for three and a half centuries in the New World did not have the ring of progress.

—Why We Can't Wait, p. 33

GENERATION GAP

The generation of the sixties, according to King, was set apart from all the previous generations and the values that had guided the generations of the past. Unique historical conditions resulted in "the alienation of young people from society," as he put it in his radio lecture on "Youth and Social Action" in 1967.

"This is the first generation to grow up in the era of the nuclear bomb, knowing that it may be the last generation of mankind. This is the generation not only of war, but of war in its ultimate revelation. This is the generation that truly has no place to hide and no place to find security."

Young people today are exposed to a "tempest of evils," said Dr. King, evils of great proportion, exposed for all to see as never before.

"The tempest of evils provides the answer for those adults who ask why this young generation is so unfathomable, so alienated, and frequently so freakish."

(see HIPPIES)

GHETTO

Contrary to the myth held by many white Americans, the ghetto is not a monolithic unit of dope addicts, alcoholics, prostitutes and unwed mothers. There are churches in the ghetto as well as bars. There are stable families in the ghetto as well as illegitimacies. Ninety percent of the young people of the ghetto never come in conflict with the law.

—*Where Do We Go from Here?* p. 113
(see BLACK FAMILY, EDUCATION, FAMILY)

GOD

King was deeply depressed when a march in which he was participating turned violent on March 28, 1968 in Memphis. Those close to him observed that they had never seen him so depressed. But the next morning King appeared at a press conference a changed man—calm, strong, eloquent, in command.

A newsman came up to him after the press conference and asked: "Dr. King, what has happened to you since last night? Have you talked with someone?"

King smiled and replied, "No. I haven't talked with anyone. I have only talked with God."

Martin Luther King talked with God frequently.

"God has been profoundly real to me in recent years," confided King in an April 1959 speech. "In the midst of outer dangers I have felt an inner calm. In the midst of lonely days and dreary nights I have heard an inner voice saying, 'Lo, I will be with you.'"

King believed in a personal God rather than an impersonal God; he believed that God was on the side of justice. These keystones of his belief were set down in *The Strength to Love:*

"I am convinced that the universe is under the control of a loving purpose, and that in the struggle for righteousness man has cosmic companionship. Behind the harsh appearances of the world there is a benign power. To say that this God is personal is not to make him a finite object beside other objects or attribute to him the limitations of human personality; it is to take what is finest and noblest in our consciousness and affirm its perfect existence in him."

King believed that God was on the side of those who struggle for freedom and justice, as long as they employed methods that were good rather than evil. Nonviolence is a method based on goodness; it is inherently good; it will inevitably lead to good results, according to King's credo. King was absolutely convinced that God would support a movement based on nonviolence. He felt he was divinely inspired to lead such a movement; he believed that God was behind it.

King was confident that God was on the side of the oppressed, not the oppressors; that God was on the side of freedom, not tyrants. King believed that the God that supported the American cause of Independence in 1776 also supported the Union cause in the Civil War and inspired the Emancipation Proclamation. King believed that the same God would support the civil rights movement—especially if nonviolent methods were employed.

It is not possible to fully understand the actions and methods of Martin Luther King in purely political or historical terms. He was not simply trying to win black people over to his cause; he was not simply trying to win white people over to his cause; he was always trying to win the support of God. In order to understand him it is necessary to understand that he was always trying to court divine favor for his cause. There were times when he took a position that he knew would cost him popularity and support, but he was more afraid of losing divine favor than of losing popularity.

Whenever a victory was achieved, King felt it was important to give credit to God. After the hardfought Birmingham campaign resulted in a great victory for the civil rights cause in May 1963, King had this to say at the press conference:

"When all is said and done, when this situation is seen in perspective of eternity, ultimate credit and glory and honor must be given to Almighty God, for He has clearly been at work among us. And it is He alone who has finally gained the victory for all His children."

Love yourself, if that means rational and healthy self-interest. You are commanded to do that. That is the length of life. . . . Love your neighbor as you love yourself. You are commanded to do that. That is the breadth of life. But never forget that there is a first and even greater commandment: "Love the Lord thy God with all thy heart and all thy soul and all thy mind." This is the height of life. And when you do this you live the complete life.

—*The Strength to Love*, p. 76

The Lord is a God of justice.

—The Strength to Love, p. 7

Whatever the name, some extra-human force labors to create a harmony out of the discords of the universe. There is a creative power that works to pull down mountains of evil and level hilltops of injustice. God still works through history His wonders to perform.

—Stride Toward Freedom, p. 70

The God that we worship is not some Aristotelian "unmoved mover" who merely contemplates upon Himself; He is not merely a self-knowing God, but an other-loving God Who forever works through history for the establishment of His kingdom.

—Prayer Pilgrimage for Freedom address,
Washington, D.C., May 17, 1957

We must be reminded anew that God is at work in his universe. He is not outside the world looking on with a sort of cold indifference.... As we struggle to defeat the forces of evil, the God of the universe struggles with us.

—The Strength to Love, p. 64

A healthy religion rises above the idea that God wills evil. Although God permits evil in order to preserve the freedom of man, he does not cause evil.

—The Strength to Love, p. 82

If God dealt with evil in the overbearing way that we wish, he would defeat his ultimate purpose. We are responsible human beings, not blind automatons; persons, not puppets. By endowing us with freedom, God relinquished a measure of his own sovereignty and imposed certain limitations upon himself. If his children are free, they must do his will by voluntary choice.

—*The Strength to Love*, p. 64

The belief that God will do everything for man is as untenable as the belief that man can do everything for himself. It, too, is based on a lack of faith. We must learn that to expect God to do everything while we do nothing is not faith but superstition.

—*The Strength to Love*, p. 123

God freely offers to do for us what we cannot do for ourselves. Our humble and openhearted acceptance is faith. So by faith we are saved. Man filled with God and God operating through man bring unbelievable changes in our individual and social lives.

—*The Strength to Love*, p. 124
(see also CHRISTIAN LOVE, EVIL,
HISTORY, LOVE, PRAYER, UNIVERSE)

GODS

There is so much frustration in the world because we have relied on gods rather than God. We have genuflected before the god of science only to find that it has given us the atomic bomb, producing fears and anxieties that science can never mitigate.

We have worshipped the god of pleasure only to discover that thrills play out and sensations are short-lived.

We have bowed before the god of money only to learn that there are such things as love and friendship that money cannot buy and that in a world of possible depressions, stock market crashes, and bad business investments, money is a rather uncertain deity.

These transitory gods are not able to save or bring happiness to the human heart. Only God is able. It is faith in him that we must discover.

—*The Strength to Love*, p. 107
(see MONEY, SCIENCE, TECHNOLOGY)

GOVERNMENT

There is a need for strong and aggressive leadership from the federal government. If the executive and legislative branches were as concerned about the protection of the citizenship rights of all people as the federal courts have been, the transition from a segregated to an integrated society would be much further along than it is today.

—*Stride Toward Freedom*, p. 198

Government action is not the whole answer to the present crisis, but it is an important partial answer. Morals cannot be legislated, but behavior can be regulated. The law cannot make an employer love me, but it can keep him from refusing to hire me because of the color of my skin.

—*Stride Toward Freedom*, p. 198

Negroes must therefore not only formulate a program; they must fashion new tactics which do not count on government goodwill but serve, instead, to compel unwilling authorities to yield to the mandates of justice.

—*The Trumpet of Conscience*, p. 14

Our government must depend more on its moral power than on its military power.

—*Where Do We Go from Here?* p. 133
(see also AMERICA, LAW)

GREATNESS

"Everybody can be great," preached Martin Luther King, "because anybody can serve."

The secret of greatness is not worldly success but worldly service.

(see SERVICE, SUCCESS)

GROUP

We have been oppressed as a group and we must overcome that oppression as a group.

—*Where Do We Go from Here?* p. 125

(see CIVIL RIGHTS, ORGANIZATION, POWER, UNITY)

GUARANTEED NATIONAL INCOME

"I am now convinced that the simplest approach will prove to be the most revolutionary," testified Dr. King at a Senate hearing on December 15, 1966.

"The solution to poverty is to abolish it directly by a now rather widely discussed measure—the guaranteed national income."

In his appearance before Senator Abraham Ribicoff's Government Operations Committee, Dr. King said the national income should be tied to a program that would provide jobs for all the unemployed who are able to work.

Previous antipoverty programs had failed, he testified, because they tried "to solve poverty by first solving another condition." The most direct approach is to guarantee jobs and income for all who need them. "Our emphasis should shift from exclusive attention to putting people to work over to enabling people to consume."

* * *

We must create full employment or we must create in-comes. People must be made consumers by one method or the other.

—*Where Do We Go from Here?* p. 163
(see BILL OF RIGHTS FOR THE DISADVANTAGED,
ECONOMIC JUSTICE, ECONOMIC REFORM, POVERTY)

H

HATRED

"Don't ever let anyone pull you so low as to hate them," King exhorted his fellow protestors in the Montgomery Bus Boycott. "We must use the weapon of love. We must have compassion and understanding for those who hate us."

Hate hurts the hater as well as the hated. The individual who hates loses some of his individuality. According to King, hatred corrupts the personality. Hatred causes disharmony within the soul, which is the source of personality. Thus hatred has a depersonalizing effect: the more we hate, the more of our personality we lose in the process.

Hate is just as injurious to the person who hates. Like an unchecked cancer, hate corrodes the personality and eats away its vital unity.

—*Where Do We Go from Here?* p. 64

Hate is rooted in fear, and the only cure for fear-hate is love.

—*The Strength to Love*, p. 112

Hatred and bitterness can never cure the disease of fear; only love can do that. Hatred paralyzes life; love releases it. Hatred confuses life; love harmonizes it. Hatred darkens life; love illuminates it.

—*The Strength to Love*, p. 114

Hate begets hate; violence begets violence; toughness begets a greater toughness. We must meet the forces of hate with the power of love; we must meet physical force with soul force.

—*Stride Toward Freedom*, p. 87

Returning hate for hate multiplies hate, adding deeper darkness to a night already devoid of stars. Darkness cannot drive out darkness; only light can do that. Hate cannot drive out hate; only love can do that.

—*The Strength to Love*, p. 37

We never get rid of an enemy by meeting hate with hate; we get rid of an enemy by getting rid of enmity.

—*The Strength to Love*, p. 38

There is some good in the worst of us and some evil in the best of us. When we discover this, we are less prone to hate our enemies.

—*The Strength to Love*, p. 35
(see EVIL, FORGIVENESS, LOVE, RETALIATION)

HEAVEN

Many have attempted to say that the ideal of a better world will be worked out in the next world. But Jesus taught men to say, "Thy will be done on earth, as it is in heaven." Although the world seems to be in a bad shape today, we must never lose faith in the power of God to achieve his purpose.

—"What a Christian Should Think
About the Kingdom of Heaven,"
in Boston Collection,
quoted in Smith and Zepp, p. 129
(see also KINGDOM OF GOD)

HIGHER SELF

"Each of us is two selves," King told his Ebenezer congregation in a sermon on the subject of evil. "And the great burden of life is to always try to keep that higher self in command. Don't let the lower self take over."

(see also DUALISM, SIN)

HIPPIES

The hippies of the 1960s called attention to themselves with their long hair, colorful clothes, rejection of conventional lifestyles, and opposition to the Vietnam War.

The hippies, according to Dr. King, "may be traced in a fairly direct line from yesterday's beatniks. The hippies are not only colorful but complex; and in many respects their extreme conduct illuminates the negative effect of society's evils on sensitive young people. . . .

"The importance of the hippies is not in their unconventional behavior, but in the fact that some hundreds of thousands of young people, in turning to a flight from reality, are expressing a profoundly discrediting judgment on the society they emerge from."

King prophesied that the hippy movement would not be an enduring one because the hippies were essentially escapists—and escape is not a viable solution.

"It seems to me that the hippies will not last long as a mass group," he predicted in his 1967 radio lecture on "Youth and Social Action." "They cannot survive because there is no solution in escape."

However, the hippies were ahead of their time in one important respect. They believed in peace, not as a distant dream, but as a practical way of life. "One dream of the hippie group is very significant, and that is its dream of peace. Most of the hippies are pacifists, and a few have thought their way through to a persuasive and psychologically sophisticated 'peace strategy.' And society at large may be more ready now to learn from that dream than it was a century or two ago, to listen to the argument for peace, not as a dream, but as a practical possibility: something to choose and use."

(see GENERATION, YOUTH)

HISTORY

"God still works through history His wonders to perform," wrote King in *Stride Toward Freedom*.

King saw history as the working out of man's relationship with God, from fear toward love, from selfishness toward community, from evil toward justice, from separation (from God and one another) toward integration (with God and one another).

"God had decided to use Montgomery as the proving ground for the struggle and the triumph of freedom and justice in America," he wrote of the Montgomery Bus Boycott. King felt it was the hand of God behind "Montgomery, the cradle of the Confederacy, being transformed into Montgomery, the cradle of freedom and justice."

During the difficult days of the Birmingham campaign, King appealed to the sense of history of the demonstrators.

"There are those who write history. There are those who make history. There are those who experience history," said King at a mass meeting on May 6, 1963 in Birmingham.

"I don't know how many of you would be able to write a history book. But you are certainly making history, and you are experiencing history. And you will make it possible for the historians of the future to write a marvelous chapter. Never in the history of this nation have so many people been arrested for the cause of freedom and human dignity."

Fortunately, history does not pose problems without eventually producing solutions. The disenchanted, the disadvantaged, and the disinherited seem, at times of deep crisis, to summon up some sort of genius that enables them to perceive and capture the appropriate weapons to carve out their destiny. Such was the peaceable weapon of nonviolent direct action.

—*Why We Can't Wait*, p. 36

This is a great hour for the Negro. The challenge is here. To become the instruments of a great idea is a privilege that history gives only occasionally. Arnold Toynbee says in *A Study of History* that it may be the Negro who will give the new spiritual dynamic to western civilization that it so desperately needs to survive.

—*Stride Toward Freedom*, p. 224

History is the story of the struggle between good and evil.

—*The Strength to Love*, p. 59

History is the story of evil forces that advance with seemingly irresistible power only to be crushed by the battling rams of the forces of justice.

—*The Strength to Love*, p. 103

History is ultimately guided by spirit, not matter.

—*Stride Toward Freedom*, p. 92

Waterloo symbolizes the doom of every Napolean and is an eternal reminder to a generation drunk with military power that in the long run of history might does not make right and the power of the sword cannot conquer the power of the spirit.

—*The Strength to Love*, p. 104

History has thrust upon our generation an indescribably important destiny—to complete a process of democratization which our nation has too long developed too slowly, but which is our most powerful weapon for world respect and emulation.

—*Stride Toward Freedom*, p. 196–97

When in future generations men look back upon these turbulent, tension-filled days through which we are passing, they will see God working through history for the salvation of man.

—*The Strength to Love*, p. 104
(see also AMERICA, EVIL, GOD, JUSTICE)

HONEYMOON

"Do you know Corrie and I spent our honeymoon in a funeral home?" It sounded like a joke, and Martin relished saying it. Actually, it was literally true of his wedding night. After the wedding ceremony at Coretta's parents' home outside Marion, Georgia, on June 18, 1953, the newlyweds set off on their honeymoon by car. They drove and drove, but couldn't find a motel with a bridal suite that would accept Negroes.

Finally they located a Mr. Robert Tubbs, a black man who owned a funeral parlor in Marion and was acquainted with Coretta's parents. Mr. and Mrs. Tubbs allowed the young newlyweds to spend the night at his establishment. Thus Martin Luther King and his bride spent their wedding night in a funeral home.

(see ARTIFICIAL FLOWERS, FIRST DATE, WEDDING)

HOOVER, J. EDGAR

"Martin Luther King is the most notorious liar in the country." Hoover made this astonishing statement, and a number of other personal attacks against Martin Luther King, at a rare press conference on November 18, 1964 in the presence of a delegation of women reporters led by Sarah McLendon. Hoover, whose highest priority was defending the FBI, was enraged by a recent published remark of King's that the FBI had not acted to curtail violence in the South because many of its agents were southerners.

It was unusual for Hoover to make a public statement. His methods were usually more secretive. On December 23, 1963, during a nine-hour session with his deputy William Sullivan, he had approved a plan to reveal King to the country "as being what he actually is—a fraud, demagogue and scoundrel" and thus "to take him off his pedestal and to reduce him completely in influence."

However, when Hoover learned that King was going to receive the 1964 Nobel Peace Prize, he was furious. He called a hasty press conference to refute King's criticism of the FBI, hoping to discredit King and thwart the award.

Responding to Hoover's attack, King sent a telegram to the FBI saying that although he had indeed questioned the institution's effectiveness, he had not attributed the problem merely to the presence of southerners on the staff. As for Hoover's accusation, King said Hoover's "inconceivable" charge must be the result of "extreme pressure." King said of Hoover: "He has apparently faltered under the awesome burdens, complexities, and responsibilities of his office. Therefore, I cannot engage in a public debate with him."

Hoover's retaliation to King's telegram was to authorize the sending of an anonymous blackmail threat to King. Sullivan was instructed to prepare a composite tape of various recordings made by hidden FBI microphones at King's motel rooms. Andrew Young, who heard the tape later, described it: "Toward the end there was a recording of somebody moanin' and groanin' as though they were in the act of sexual intercourse, but it didn't sound like anybody I knew, and certainly not Martin." Enclosed with the tape was a letter, drafted by Sullivan, urging King to forgo the Nobel Prize and commit suicide.

"King, look into your heart," said the letter. "You know you are a complete fraud and a greater liability to all of us Negroes. . . .

"King, like all frauds your end is approaching. . . . You are done. . . . The American public, the church organizations that have been helping—Protestants, Catholics and Jews will know you for what you are—an evil beast. So will others who have backed you. You are done.

"King, there is only one thing left for you to do. You know what it is. You have just 34 days in which to do it. . . . You are done. There is but one way out for you. You better take it before your filthy self is bared to the nation."

When King received the tape and the accompanying letter he knew immediately that Hoover was behind it. He ignored the threat and accepted the Nobel Prize.

(see COMMUNISTS, FBI, LEVISON)

HOPE

When hopes are met with delay or defeat, it is hard to keep hope alive. But it is even harder to live without hope.

"One of the most agonizing problems within our human experience is that few, if any, of us live to see our fondest hopes fulfilled," wrote King in *The Strength to Love.* "The hopes of our childhood and the promises of our mature years are unfinished symphonies."

When hope diminishes, the hate element is often turned toward those who originally built up the hope.

—Sermon, "Who Is My Neighbor?" February 18, 1968

We must accept finite disappointment, but we must never lose infinite hope.

—*The Strength to Love,* p. 83
(see GOD, UNIVERSE)

HUMAN BEINGS

We see men as Jews or Gentiles, Catholics or Protestants, Chinese or American, Negroes or whites. We fail to think of them as fellow human beings made from the same basic stuff as we, molded in the same divine image.

—*The Strength to Love,* p. 19
(see BROTHERHOOD, IMAGE OF GOD, PERSONALITY)

HUMAN NATURE

There is within human nature an amazing potential for goodness.

—"Love, Law and Civil Disobedience,"
New South, vol. 16, December 1961, p. 6

We must never forget that there is something within human nature that can respond to goodness . . . the image of God is never totally gone . . . there is something within human nature that can be changed, and this stands at the top of . . . the philosophy of nonviolence.

—"Love, Law and Civil Disobedience,"
New South, vol. 16, December 1961, p. 7
(see COMPASSION, MAN, NONVIOLENCE, PERSONALITY)

HUMAN WORTH

The worth of the individual does not lie in the measure of his intellect, his racial origin or his social position. Human worth lies in relatedness to God.

—*Where Do We Go from Here?* p. 97
(see GOD, PERSONALITY)

HUMOR

Great eloquence is never devoid of humor. Wit is the far side of wisdom. The humorous, playful side of Martin Luther King was not known to the public, but it was known to those close to him.

"He did have another side," wrote Ralph Abernathy in his memoirs, "and those of us who knew him well enjoyed his company in a way that outsiders could never understand. Martin was fun-loving, and when he was offstage you could usually find him telling a joke or teasing somebody. He had a perfect sense of timing and he instinctively knew what was funny. Some people have that gift and some people don't. He had it. I'm convinced that if he had wanted to be a standup comic he could have been almost as famous in that role."

King was playful to the very end of his life. A few hours before his assassination he got into a pillow fight with Andrew Young. He pretended to be angry with Young, chastising him about not reporting back sooner; suddenly he struck with a pillow. They fought until feathered down was flying and they collapsed with laughter. Later that afternoon Martin played a prank on his mother. He and his brother A. D. called their mother on the telephone and "switched voices," each pretending to be the other. They fooled her for a couple of minutes, but then she burst out laughing when she realized she was being put on.

(see AGE, ICE CREAM, NEW YORK NIGHTCAP, SHOES, SNORE)

I

ICE CREAM

King was a connoisseur of good food, good cooking, and especially ice cream. The following incident illustrates his playful side.

One night he was a dinner guest at Ralph Abernathy's house and, at the conclusion of a satisfying meal, was devouring a dessert of homemade ice cream prepared by Abernathy's wife, Juanita. Somewhere in the middle of the second bowl of ice cream, King was struck by inspiration. He turned to Juanita and flourished his spoon, "Juanita, I believe we can solve this whole boycott problem if we carry a bowl of this ice cream over to George Wallace," he said referring to the segregationist governor of Alabama. "I think I'll take it over right now."

King rose, picked up the bowl, and eyed it for awhile. His hosts broke into laughter while he hesitated, acting as though he were mesmerized by the tantalizing temptation of the ice cream. Reconsidering, he sat back down in his chair and loaded up his spoon. "No. He doesn't deserve it. I'm just going to sit here and eat it myself."

(see AGE, HUMOR, NEW YORK NIGHTCAP, SHOES, SNORE)

IMAGE OF GOD

Deeply rooted in our religious heritage is the conviction that every man is an heir to a legacy of dignity and worth. Our Judeo-Christian tradition refers to this inherent dignity of man in the biblical term the *image of God*. The innate worth referred to in the phrase, the *image of God*, is universally shared in equal portions by all men.

—Speech, "Man in a Revolutionary World," 1965
(see HUMAN WORTH, PERSONALITY)

INDIA

"To other countries I may go as a tourist, but to India I come as a pilgrim," King informed reporters on his arrival in New Delhi in February 1959. He was given a hero's welcome. Crowds gathered around the "Negro Gandhian" who had taken over from Gandhi the torch of nonviolent direct action.

At his farewell press conference before departing from India on March 9, Dr. King offered a proposal to the Indian nation. He suggested that India be true to Gandhi's principles and lead the world in disarmament.

"It may be that just as India had to take the lead and show the world that national independence could be achieved nonviolently, so India may have to take the lead and call for universal disarmament, and if no other nation will join her immediately, India should declare itself for disarmament unilaterally."

This proposal was not well-received. King was criticized for being naive, meddlesome, and ignorant of practical realities: all the usual objections. A triumphant pilgrimage

to India ended on a sour note when King urged the coun-
trymen of Gandhi to live up to their nonviolent national
heritage.

(see Biography 1959, DISARMAMENT, GANDHI)

INFERIORITY COMPLEX

We often develop inferiority complexes and we stumble
through life with a feeling of insecurity, a lack of self-
confidence, and a sense of impending failure. A fear of
what life may bring encourages some persons to wander
aimlessly along the frittering road of excessive drink and
sexual promiscuity. I know this. I know it from my own
personal experience.

—Sermon, "Mastering Our Fears," Atlanta, Georgia,
September 10, 1967
(see SELF-ESTEEM)

INJUNCTIONS

"I have so many injunctions I don't even look at them
anymore," declared Dr. King when he arrived in Danville,
Illinois, on June 11, 1963 to lead a demonstration in defi-
ance of a local injunction.

If King had called off every peace march, demonstration, or freedom walk that had a local court injunction
pending against it, he would have participated in very few
civil rights events.

"I was enjoined January 15, 1929," said Martin Luther
King, "when I was born in the United States a Negro."

INJUSTICE

In the summer of 1966 King led demonstrations in white
neighborhoods of Chicago. He was accused, as he had

been so many times before, of inviting violence with his provocative tactics. Once again he gave his answer:

"We do not seek to precipitate violence. However, we are aware that the existence of injustice in society is the existence of violence—latent violence. We feel we must constantly expose this evil, even if it brings violence upon us."

Injustices to the Negro must be brought out into the open where they cannot be evaded.

—*Playboy* Interviews, 1967, p. 356

Like a boil that can never be cured so long as it is covered up but must be opened with all its ugliness to the natural medicines of air and light, injustice must be exposed, with all the tension its exposure creates, to the light of human conscience and the air of national opinion before it can be cured.

—Letter from Birmingham Jail, 1963

Every act of injustice mars and defaces the image of God in man.

—*Where Do We Go from Here?* p. 99

To accept passively an unjust system is to cooperate with that system; thereby the oppressed become as evil as the oppressor.

—*Stride Toward Freedom*, p. 212

Injustice anywhere is a threat to justice everywhere. We are caught in an inescapable network of mutuality, tied in a single garment of destiny. Whatever affects one directly, affects all indirectly.

—Letter from Birmingham Jail, 1963
(see CRISIS, EVIL, EXPOSURE, JUSTICE, MASS MEDIA, TENSION)

INTEGRATION

What is needed is a strategy for change, a tactical program that will bring the Negro into the mainstream of American life as quickly as possible.

Where Do We Go from Here? p. 59

Integration is creative, and is therefore more profound and far-reaching than desegregation. Integration is the positive acceptance of desegregation and the welcomed participation of Negroes into the total range of human activities.

—"The Ethical Demands of Integration,"
Religion and Labor, May 1963, p. 4

It is one thing to agree that the goal of integration is morally and legally right; it is another thing to commit oneself positively and actively to the ideal of integration—the former is intellectual assent, the latter is actual belief. These are days that demand practices to match professions. This is no day to pay lip service to integration, we must pay *life* service to it.

—*Stride Toward Freedom*, p. 200

Indeed it is the keystone of my faith in the future that we will someday achieve a thoroughly integrated society. I believe that before the turn of the century, if trends continue to move and develop as presently, we will have moved a long, long way toward such a society.

—"An Interview with Martin Luther King,"
Playboy, January 1965, p. 128

On the one hand, integration is true intergroup, interpersonal living. On the other hand, it is the mutual sharing of power.

—*Where Do We Go from Here?* p. 62

Our ultimate goal is integration which is genuine inter-group and interpersonal living. Only through nonviolence can this goal be attained, for the aftermath of nonviolence is reconciliation and the creation of the beloved community.

—*Stride Toward Freedom*, p. 220
(see also BELOVED COMMUNITY, DESEGREGATION, SYNTHESIS)

INTERDEPENDENCE

All men are interdependent. Every nation is an heir of a vast treasury of ideas and labor to which both the living and the dead of all nations have contributed. Whether we realize it or not, each of us lives eternally "in the red." We are everlasting debtors to known and unknown men and women. When we arise in the morning, we go into the bathroom where we reach for a sponge which is provided for us by a Pacific islander. We reach for soap that is created for us by a European. Then at the table we drink coffee which is provided for us by a South American, or tea by a Chinese, or cocoa by a West African. Before we leave for our jobs we are already beholden to more than half the world.

—*Where Do We Go from Here?* p. 181
(see BROTHERHOOD, HUMAN BEINGS, INTERRELATED, WORLD PERSPECTIVE)

INTERNAL VERSUS EXTERNAL

Every man lives in two realms, the internal and the external. The internal is that realm of spiritual ends expressed in art, literature, morals, and religion. The external is that complex of devices, techniques, mechanisms, and instrumentalities by means of which we live. Our problem today is that we have allowed the internal to become lost in the external. We have allowed the means by which we live to outdistance the ends for which we live.

—*The Strength to Love*, p. 52

INTERRACIAL MARRIAGE

King fell into a conversation with a white woman who proclaimed she was very liberal and lacked any prejudice against blacks. She was all for equal rights, she said, but she confessed she wouldn't want her daughter to marry a black man.

"This lady could not see that her failure to accept intermarriage negated her claim to genuine liberalism," wrote King later in *Where Do We Go from Here?* "She failed to see that implicit in her rejection was the feeling that her daughter had some pure superior nature that should not be contaminated by the impure, inferior nature of the Negro.

"The question of intermarriage is never raised in a society cured of the disease of racism."

Marriage is an individual matter that must be decided on the merits of individual cases. Properly speaking, races do not marry; individuals marry.

—*Stride Toward Freedom*, p. 206

The Negro's primary aim is to be the white man's brother, not his brother-in-law.

—*Stride Toward Freedom*, p. 206
(see INTEGRATION, SYNTHESIS)

INTERRELATED

In a real sense all life is interrelated. The agony of the poor impoverishes the rich; the betterment of the poor enriches the rich. We are inevitably our brother's keeper because we are our brother's brother. Whatever affects one directly affects all indirectly.

—*Where Do We Go from Here?* p. 181

I can never be what I ought to be until you are what you ought to be, and you can never be what you ought to be until I am what I ought to be. This is the interrelated structure of reality.

The Strength to Love, p. 54

Centuries ago, civilization acquired the certain knowledge that man had emerged from barbarity only to the degree that he recognized his relatedness to his fellow man.

—*Why We Can't Wait*, p. 128
(see ALIENATION, INTERDEPENDENCE)

J

JAIL

When King was arrested and thrown into a cell in Montgomery City Jail during the bus boycott, he was soon surrounded by other prisoners, all of whom were eager to talk to him. One prisoner asked if King could help get him out. Then another prisoner asked if King would help free him. A third prisoner asked the same thing of King.

King turned to the group and said: "Fellows, before I can assist any of you in getting out, I've got to get *myself* out." At this they all laughed. It was only then that they realized their leader was a prisoner, too.

(see PRISON)

JEWS

I solemnly pledge to do my utmost to uphold the fair name of the Jews. Not only because we need their friend-

ship, and surely we do, but mainly because bigotry in any form is an affront to us all.

—"Of Riots and Wrongs Against the Jews,"
SCLC Newsletter, July–August 1964, p. 11

JIM CROW

"We had a big funeral last weekend," announced Martin Luther King to the Philosophical Club at Boston University as he arrived for its weekly meeting. "We buried Jim."

The pipe-smoking black graduate students who convened one evening a week in the early 1950s to discuss philosophical issues glanced up in surprise at King, their founder and chief philosopher.

"Jim who?"

"Jim Crow," drawled King, citing the slang name for segregation. They laughed, realizing he was joking. "Yeah, we did Jim up real good. We put him to rest."

A few years later they realized he wasn't joking after all.

(see DESEGREGATION, HUMOR)

JOHNSON, LYNDON BAINES

During their first meeting at the White House, the newly sworn in President Johnson declined to be photographed with Martin Luther King. That set the tone for their relationship, which was cordial but not friendly.

King held a reluctant admiration for some of John Kennedy's personal attributes, but this admiration did not extend to JFK's successor. King described the contrast between the Kennedy style of leadership and the Johnson style this way: "When you met with the Kennedys, you did most of the talking and they listened. When you met with the Johnson people, they did the talking and you listened."

Nevertheless, Johnson demonstrated an immediate will-

ingness to commit himself to passing civil rights legislation, and with more Congressional support than Kennedy
ever enjoyed, Johnson was able to pass more civil rights
legislation than Kennedy had ever proposed. It was during the Johnson administration that Kennedy's Civil
Rights Bill was passed in 1964. It was during the Johnson
administration that the Voting Rights Act was passed in
1965. It was during the first two years of the Johnson administration that the civil rights movement reached its
peak with a paroxysm of legislation before the national
priority turned toward Vietnam.

When President Johnson appeared on television to urge
the swift passage of the Voting Rights Act of 1965, Martin
Luther King was moved to tears.

"It is the effort of American Negroes to secure for themselves the full blessings of American life," said President
Johnson in a speech to Congress on March 15, 1965, which
he later recalled as one of his proudest moments. "Their
cause must be our cause, too. Because it is not just Negroes, but really it is all of us who must overcome the
crippling legacy of bigotry and injustice." Then, pausing
dramatically after each word, the president concluded:
"We . . . shall . . . overcome!"

Hearing the president recite the refrain of the song that
had largely through King's efforts become the anthem of
the civil rights movement brought tears to King's eyes as
he watched in the living room of Mrs. Jimmie Lee Jackson
in Selma, Alabama. "Martin told us that no speech by a
white man had ever moved him before," recalled one of
his aides later, "but now he felt the Negro cause was actually going to succeed."

That night King called President Johnson to congratulate him. Richard Goodwin, who had written the speech,
was in the room with Johnson when the President took the
call. "Thank you, Reverend, but you're the leader who's
making it all possible, I'm just following along trying to

do what's right." Johnson hung up and turned to Goodwin. "That was King. He said it was ironic that after a century, a southern white president would help lead the way toward the salvation of the Negro."

The relationship between President Johnson and Martin Luther King turned sour soon afterward when King declared his opposition to the Vietnam War. King felt that Johnson's Vietnam policy was due in part to a personality flaw. Unlike John Kennedy, who was capable of admitting error—as in the Bay of Pigs fiasco—Johnson could not admit any error, King wrote. "Lyndon Johnson seems to be unable to make this kind of statesmanlike gesture in connection with Vietnam."

Johnson regarded King's antiwar stance as a personal betrayal. "How is it possible," Johnson said, "that all these people could be so ungrateful to me after I had given them so much? Take the Negroes. I fought for them. . . . I spilled my guts out in getting those civil rights bills through Congress. . . . I asked so little in return. Just a little thanks, just a little appreciation. But look what I got instead."

Black leadership was split over the Vietnam issue and King was accused of antagonizing the President. At one meeting of black civil rights leaders in March 1967, Whitney Young of the Urban League defended the war. Young told King his criticism of the war was unwise for it would make an enemy of President Johnson.

King, as angry as his companions ever remember seeing him, replied, "Whitney, what you're saying may get you a foundation grant, but it won't get you into the kingdom of truth!"

(see EISENHOWER, KENNEDY, JOHN F., NIXON, VIETNAM WAR)

JOY

When the soul returns to its true home, there is always joy.

—*The Strength to Love*, p. 92

JUDEO-CHRISTIAN HERITAGE

I am happy to say that the nonviolent movement in America has come not from secular forces but from the heart of the Negro church. . . . The great principles of love and justice which stand at the center of the nonviolent movement are deeply rooted in our Judeo-Christian heritage.

—Speech to National Conference on Religion and Race, 1963
(see CHRISTIAN LOVE, GOD, LOVE, JUSTICE, NONVIOLENCE)

JUDGMENT OF GOD

Now the Judgment of God is upon us, and we must either learn to live together as brothers or we are going to perish together as fools.

—*The Trumpet of Conscience*, p. 68
(see WAR)

JUSTICE

For King justice was the critical issue of earthly life. Justice was more than a legal issue; it was more than a moral issue; it was a spiritual issue. The realization of justice was the realization of God's presence on earth. "The Lord God is a god of justice," he asserted.

Justice is the same for all issues; it cannot be categorized. It is not possible to be in favor of justice for some people and not be in favor of justice for all people. Justice cannot be divided.

* * *

Justice is indivisible.

—*The Trumpet of Conscience*, p. 24

I think this is what Jesus meant when he looked at his disciples one day and said, "I come not to bring peace but a sword." Now certainly he didn't mean he came to bring a physical sword. Certainly he didn't mean that he did not come to bring true peace. But Jesus was saying in substance: ... whenever I come, a conflict is precipitated between the old and the new. Whenever I come, tension sets in between justice and injustice.

—Speech, "True Peace,"
Atlanta, at outset of bus boycott, July 5, 1962

The Negro revolt is evolving into more than a quest for desegregation and equality. It is a challenge to a system that has created miracles of production and technology to create justice.

—*The Trumpet of Conscience*, pp. 16–17

Justice at its best is love correcting everything that stands against love.

—*Where Do We Go from Here?* p. 90

Justice is really love in calculation.

—Speech, Montgomery, Alabama, December 5, 1955
(see INJUSTICE, LAW, LOVE, PEACE)

KENNEDY, JOHN F.

A simple phone call made by John Kennedy to Coretta King may have been the decisive factor in the 1960 presidential election. The phone call itself was very brief. It lasted only a few seconds. John Kennedy, in the final days of the campaign, was running neck-and-neck with Richard Nixon. When Kennedy heard about King's four-month prison sentence in Reidsville State Prison in Georgia he impulsively called Coretta King, who was at home in Atlanta, pregnant.

Coretta was quite surprised to answer the phone and hear a voice say, "Just a moment, Mrs. King, for Senator Kennedy." A few seconds later she heard the famous Boston accent.

"I want to express to you my concern about your husband," said JFK. "I know this must be very hard for you. I understand you are expecting a baby."

"Yes, in three months," said Mrs. King.

"I just wanted you to know that I was thinking about

you and Dr. King. If there is anything I can do to help, please feel free to call on me."

That was it. It was simply a gesture. But it was a gesture made by one candidate and not the other.

John Kennedy received a lot of the credit when Dr. King was released from Reidsville Prison a few days later. Actually it was his brother and campaign manager Robert Kennedy who called Judge Mitchell (the judge responsible for King's sentence) and persuaded him to release King on bail. John Kennedy did not authorize his brother's actions; he was not aware of them. The younger Kennedy was acting independently in intervening to obtain King's release. Nevertheless, the phone call to Coretta and King's subsequent release rallied the black vote overwhelmingly in favor of John Kennedy.

Although Martin Luther King, Jr., did not formally endorse any candidate, his father, Martin Luther King, Sr., made an emotional endorsement to his congregation in Atlanta: "I had expected to vote against Senator Kennedy because of his religion. But now he can be my president, Catholic or whatever he is. Any man who can take the tears away from my daughter-in-law's eyes is a good man in my book. It took courage for him to call her when he did. He has the moral courage to stand up for what is right. I've got a suitcase of votes and I'm going to go up there and dump them in John Kennedy's lap!"

The text of the senior King's sermon was later printed in a pamphlet by Harris Wofford ("No Comment Nixon Versus a Candidate with a Heart, Senator Kennedy"), and two million copies were printed and distributed in the last days of the campaign.

In a tight election, almost all of the major constituencies, men and women, Catholics and Protestants, Republicans and Democrats, were fairly evenly split between Kennedy and Nixon. The only group to provide Kennedy with an overwhelming plurality were the black voters. Because

Kennedy's margin of victory was only 112,881 votes, there are many historians who contend that the black vote made the difference, and it was the Kennedy handling of King's arrest that determined the black vote.

(see BIRMINGHAM JAIL, COMMUNISTS,
EMANCIPATION PROCLAMATION, MARCH ON WASHINGTON)

KENNEDY ASSASSINATION, JOHN F.

When President John F. Kennedy was assassinated in Dallas on November 22, 1963, King was at home in Atlanta. He learned of the assassination from a television news bulletin.

Coretta remembers that he called to her from the living room. She came in and saw him staring at the television, transfixed by the news from Dallas that was sending shockwaves around the nation.

"This is going to happen to me, too," said King. "I just realized it. This is what is going to happen to me also. I keep telling you, this is a sick society." Coretta turned and looked at her husband, horrified. "It's true, Corrie. I'll never see my fortieth birthday."

She recalled this moment later: "I was not able to say anything. I had no word to comfort my husband. I could not say, 'It won't happen to you.' I felt he was right. It was a painfully agonizing silence. I moved closer to him and gripped his hand in mine."

When reporters came to the door asking Dr. King for his views about the assassination, he issued this statement: "In mourning President Kennedy we mourn a man who had become the pride of the nation. But we also mourn for ourselves, for we know now that we are sick."

Watching the funeral with his parents, six-year-old Marty looked up at his father and said, "Daddy, President Kennedy was your best friend, wasn't he?" King smiled sadly. "He was a good friend."

President Kennedy was a strongly contrasted personality. there were, in fact, two John Kennedys. One presided in the first two years under pressure of the uncertainty caused by his razor-thin margin of victory. . . . However, in 1963, a new Kennedy had emerged. He had found that public opinion was not in a rigid mold. American political thought was not committed to conservatism, nor radicalism, nor moderation. It was above all fluid. . . . Affirmative leadership could guide it into constructive channels.

—*Why We Can't Wait*, p. 144

His last speech on race relations was the most earnest, human and profound appeal for understanding and justice that any President has uttered since the first days of the Republic. Uniting his flair for leadership with a program of social progress, he was at his death undergoing a transformation from a hesitant leader with unsure goals to a strong figure with deeply appealing objectives.

—*Why We Can't Wait*, p. 144

While the question of "who killed President Kennedy" is important, the question "what killed him" is more important. . . .

It is a climate where men cannot disagree without being disagreeable, and where they express their disagreement through violence and murder. It is the same climate that murdered Medgar Evers in Mississippi and six innocent children in Birmingham, Alabama. So in a sense we are all participants in that horrible act that tarnished the image of our nation. . . . We have created an atmosphere in which violence and hatred have become popular pastimes.

—"It's a Difficult Thing to Teach a President," *Look*, November 17, 1964
(see ASSASSINATION, BACKLASH)

On the evening of Martin Luther King's assassination, April 4, 1968, presidential candidate Senator Robert Kennedy was scheduled for a campaign rally in an Indianapolis ghetto. Riots had broken out in black communities across the nation, and Senator Kennedy was advised to cancel the appearance. He was warned that his life would be in danger and the police could not protect him adequately. But he refused to cancel. He wanted to say something to the people about the assassination. He stood in the back of a flatbed truck and faced the restless crowd:

"For those of you who are black and are tempted to be filled with hatred and distrust at the injustice of such an act, against all white people, I would only say that I can also feel in my own heart the same kind of feeling. I had a member of my family killed, but he was killed by a white man."

Robert Kennedy's aides looked at one another in shock, for none of them had ever heard him mention his brother's assassination in public before.

"We can move in that direction as a country, in great polarization—black people amongst black, white people amongst white, filled with hatred against one another.

"Or we can make an effort, as Martin Luther King did, to understand, and to comprehend, and to replace that violence, that stain of bloodshed that has spread across our land, with compassion and love."

A somber silence fell over the audience. The crowd dispersed peacefully, its anger transmuting into other emotions, more introspective and inward-turned. Six weeks later, on June 5, 1968, Robert Kennedy was assassinated in the kitchen of the Ambassador Hotel in Los Angeles after winning the California democratic primary.

"There was always a strange kind of affection between Bobby Kennedy and Dr. King," wrote Andrew Young, "a genuine spiritual brotherhood which leaped across the widest chasms of our time. If there is an afterlife, and I have no doubt there is, I am sure they are together— finally able to share the much denied love that could never be fulfilled in a world such as ours."

(see COOLING OFF, FREEDOM RIDERS, LAW)

KINGDOM OF GOD

Jesus took over the phrase "the Kingdom of God," but he changed its meaning. He refused entirely to be the kind of a Messiah that his contemporaries expected. Jesus made love the mark of sovereignty. Here we are left with no doubt as to Jesus' meaning. The Kingdom of God will be a society in which men and women live as children of God should live. It will be a kingdom controlled by the law of love.

—"What a Christian Should Think
About the Kingdom of God,"
in Boston Collection,
quoted in Smith and Zepp

Although man's moral pilgrimage may never reach a destination point on earth, his never-ceasing strivings may bring him ever closer to the city of righteousness. And though the Kingdom of God may remain *not yet* as a universal reality in history, in the present it may exist in such isolated forms as in judgment, in personal devotion, and in some group life.

—*The Strength to Love*, p. 51

L

LATE

While touring Georgia during the Poor People's Campaign in March 1968, King lagged behind schedule because of engine trouble in his chartered airplane. Arriving several hours late for a scheduled appearance in Macomb, he apologized to the audience with a sheepish grin: "I would rather be Martin Luther King late than the late Martin Luther King."

LAW

King's attitude toward the law was illustrated by this episode. On September 3, 1958 he was arrested on the steps of the courthouse in Montgomery, Alabama, on a trumped-up charge of loitering. The arresting officers handled him roughly, in full view of many witnesses, and dragged him away.

Dr. King was found guilty of disturbing the peace. Standing before Judge Eugene Loe on September 5, in front of a crowded courtroom, King made this statement:

"Your honor, you have found me guilty. My wife and I have talked and prayed over the course of action in the event this should happen. If I am fined, I must tell you that I can not in all good conscience pay a fine for an act I did not commit and for brutal treatment that I did not deserve. I am inwardly compelled to take this stand. We are commanded to resist evil by the God that created us all."

The judge was visibly irritated, for he was not accustomed to being lectured to, especially not by a black man.

"Although I cannot pay a fine, I will willingly accept the alternative which you provide, without malice," continued King. "I make this decision because of my deep concern for the injustices and indignities that my people continue to experience. I also make this decision because of my love for America and the sublime principles of liberty and equality upon which she is founded. I have come to see that America is in danger of losing her soul. Something must happen to awaken the dozing soul of America before it is too late."

Judge Loe imposed a two-week jail sentence, but King was soon released when Police Commissioner Clyde Sellers, embarrassed by the entire episode, paid his fine. Sellers said he wanted "to save the taxpayers the expense of feeding King for fourteen days."

This incident shows that King felt it was important to resist unjust laws, but that it was also important to accept the penalty for doing so. It was the acceptance of the penalty, he felt, that separated the activist who practices civil disobedience from the anarchist or the lawbreaker. The willingness to accept the penalty for breaking the unjust law is what makes civil disobedience a moral act and not merely an act of lawbreaking. "There comes a time when a moral man can't obey a law which his conscience tells him is unjust. And the important thing is that when he does that, he willingly accepts the penalty—because if he refuses to accept the penalty, then he becomes reckless, and he becomes an anarchist."

Having accepted the punishment of the law, King therefore felt fully entitled to the protection of the law. For example, on May 10, 1961, he found himself trapped inside the First Baptist Church of Montgomery with twelve hundred blacks, surrounded by an angry crowd of several thousand whites who were threatening to burn the church down. As bricks hurled by racists smashed through the stained-glass windows, King spoke to the congregation of the law's protection:

"Let us never succumb to the temptation of believing that legislation and judicial decrees play only minor roles. Morality cannot be legislated, but behavior can be regulated. Judicial decrees may not change the heart, but they can restrain the heartless.

"The law may not be able to make a man love me, but it can keep him from lynching me!"

That night King placed a phone call from the church to Attorney General Robert Kennedy, the nation's top-ranking law enforcement official, and asked for protection. The Attorney General sent seven hundred federal marshals to escort King and his companions to safety.

The law cannot make an employer love an employee, but it can prevent him from refusing to hire me because of the color of my skin. The habits, if not the hearts of people, have been and are being altered by legislative acts, judicial decisions, and executive orders. Let us not be misled by those who argue that segregation cannot be ended by force of law.

—"The Ethical Demands of Integration,"
Religion and Labor, May 1963

One may well ask: "How can you advocate breaking some laws and obeying others?" The answer lies in the fact that

135

there are two types of laws: just and unjust. I would be the first to advocate obeying just laws. One has not only a legal but a moral responsibility to obey just laws. Conversely, one has a moral responsibility to disobey unjust laws.

—Letter from Birmingham Jail, 1963

How does one determine whether a law is just or unjust? A just law is a man-made code that squares with the moral law or the law of God. An unjust law is a code that is out of harmony with the moral law.

—Letter from Birmingham Jail, 1963

An unjust law is a code that a numerical or power majority group compels a minority group to obey but does not make binding on itself. This is *difference* made legal. By the same token, a just law is a code that a majority compels a minority to follow and that it is willing to follow itself.

—Letter from Birmingham Jail, 1963

Man-made laws assure justice, but a higher law produces love. No code of conduct ever compelled a father to love his children.

—Speech, Nashville, Tennessee, December 27, 1962

Laws only declare rights; they do not deliver them. The oppressed must take hold of laws and transform them into effective mandates.

—*Where Do We Go from Here?* p. 158
(see CIVIL DISOBEDIENCE, INJUSTICE, JUSTICE)

LAW AND ORDER

Law and order exist for the purpose of establishing justice . . . when they fail in this purpose they become the danger-

ously structured dams that block the flow of social progress.

—Letter from Birmingham Jail, 1963

LEADER

I decide on the basis of conscience. A genuine leader
doesn't reflect consensus, he molds consensus.

—Statement to Chicago Real Estate Board, August 17, 1966
(see CONFORMISM, MAJORITY, NONCONFORMISM)

LEGAL QUESTIONS

In the winter of 1966 Dr. King was in Chicago trying to at-
tract national attention to the problem of urban slum conditions. He orchestrated the takeover of a slum tenement
by three civil rights groups in "trusteeship" to collect the
rent for a tenement owned by John Bender at 3738 North
Kenmore Avenue.

The action gained national publicity. Photos of King, his
wife, and others in overalls, shoveling refuse, appeared in
newspapers all over the United States.

Chicago officials were embarrassed by King's latest
"publicity stunt" and attacked it on legal grounds. "I don't
think it is legal; it is theft," said Judge James B. Parson,
himself a black man. "Laws that might be suspected to be
unconstitutional because they are discriminatory should
be attacked in the courts."

King refused to be drawn into a legal debate over legal
technicalities. He kept the debate focused on the larger
moral issues. "I won't say that it is illegal, but I would call
it supralegal," he told the *Chicago Tribune*. "The moral
question is far more important than the legal one."

(see CIVIL DISOBEDIENCE, LAW)

LETTER FROM BIRMINGHAM JAIL

The single most complete statement of Martin Luther King's principles can be found in the Letter from Birmingham Jail, dated April 16, 1963, written while in solitary confinement in Birmingham. It was a response to a published statement by eight white Alabama clergymen criticizing King's Birmingham civil disobedience campaign. "My Dear Fellow Clergymen," the letter began, "While confined here in the Birmingham city jail, I came across your recent statement calling my present activities 'unwise and untimely.' "

As King described it later, the letter "was composed under somewhat constricting circumstances. Begun on the margins of the newspaper in which the statement appeared while I was in jail, the letter was continued on scraps of writing paper supplied by a friendly Negro trusty, and concluded on a pad my attorneys were eventually permitted to leave me."

King asked Clarence Jones to smuggle out sections of the letter, much of which was written on the scattered white spaces of a rolled-up newspaper. "I'm writing this letter," he told Jones. "I want you to try to get it out, if you can."

Jones was baffled, for he felt there was more pressing business than a letter of rebuttal to some unsympathetic white clergymen. But King showed him how to follow the meandering trail of arrows across newspaper ads and wedding announcements to read the text.

No one knew it yet, but King's Letter from Birmingham Jail was one of the masterpieces of American letters, a document of enduring literary and historical value. King concluded the letter with a characteristic apology for its length.

"Never before have I written so long a letter. I'm afraid it is much too long to take your precious time. I can assure you that it would have been much shorter if I had been writing from a comfortable desk, but what else can one do when he is alone in a narrow jail cell, other than write long letters, think long thoughts, and pray long prayers?"

(see CIVIL DISOBEDIENCE, LAW, MODERATES, WAIT)

LEVISON, STANLEY

King's lifelong friendship with Stanley Levison, an idealistic white lawyer who donated his services free of charge, nevertheless cost King dearly. FBI Director J. Edgar Hoover was convinced that Levison was a communist and that King, because he was under Levison's influence, was under communist influence.

Even after President Kennedy, under pressure from Hoover, asked King to disassociate himself from Levison, King refused to do so. Levison did not share King's religious beliefs, but he and King shared certain ideals.

King would call Levison almost every night. Usually they discussed politics, but sometimes they argued about religion. It was inconceivable to King that a man as idealistic as Levison could have no belief in God. "You believe in God, Stan," he kidded Levison. "You just don't know it."

(see COMMUNISTS, HOOVER)

LOVE

At a mass meeting in Birmingham on May 6, 1963, King expounded his philosophy of love. He cited three words for love in the Greek New Testament, expressing three types of love: eros, philia, and agape.

"You've got to love the white man. God knows he needs our love. Now let me say to you that I'm not talking about emotional warmth when I talk about love. I'm not talking about sentimental emotion. But let me tell you what I mean when I say love. Now there are three words in the language of love. And I'm not trying to talk over anybody's head. I'm trying to get at a basic truth here.

"There is a word *eros*. A Greek word. That word means love. But it means a sort of romantic love. You know this is the kind of love that you have for your mate. Romantic love is inevitably a little selfish. You love your lover because there is something about your lover that *moves* you."

King's coy expression drew a big laugh from the crowd.

"That's eros. It may be the way he or she talks or the way he or she walks or the personality or the physical beauty or the intellectual power—or any of that—but it's always based on that there's something that attracts *you*. That's eros.

"Now the Greek language has another word. *Philia*. Which is a sort of intimate affection between personal friends. These are the people that you like. It's a reciprocal love. You love because you are loved. You love the people that you like. People that you like to sit down at the table and eat dinner with. People that you dial the phone and talk to. The people that you go out with. This is friendship.

"Then the Greek language comes out with another word, my friends, and I don't want you to forget it. The word is *agape*. Agape is more than romantic love. Agape is more than friendship. Agape is understanding. It is creative and redeeming good will toward all men. It is the love of God operating in the human heart. It is the overflowing love which seeks nothing in return. And when you rise to love on this level, you love people who don't move you. You love those that you don't like. You love those whose ways are distasteful to you. You love every man because God loves him.

"Now this is what I'm talking about in race relations. I

140

can't like Mr. Connor but Jesus says love him and love is greater than like."

I have discovered that the highest good is love. This principle is at the center of the cosmos. It is the great unifying force of life. God is love.

—*The Strength to Love*, p. 133

When I speak of love, I am speaking of that force which all the great religions have seen as the supreme unifying principle of life. Love is the key that unlocks the door which leads to the ultimate reality.

—*Where Do We Go from Here?* p. 191

Love is mankind's most potent weapon for personal and social transformation.

—*The Strength to Love*, p. 23

I had come to see early that the Christian doctrine of love operating through the Gandhian method of nonviolence was one of the most potent weapons available to the Negro in his struggle for freedom.

—*Stride Toward Freedom*, p. 84–85

Love that does not satisfy justice is no love at all. It is merely a sentimental affectation, little more than what one would have for a pet. Love at its best is justice concretized.

—*Where Do We Go from Here?* p. 89–90

Power without love is reckless and abusive and . . . love without power is sentimental and anemic. Power at its best is love implementing the demands of justice.

—*Where Do We Go from Here?* p. 90
(see also CHRISTIAN LOVE, FORGIVENESS, GANDHI, GOD, JUSTICE)

LOYALTIES

If we are to have peace on earth, our loyalties must become ecumenical rather than sectional. Our loyalties must transcend our race, our tribe, our class, and our nation; and this means we must develop a world perspective.

—*The Trumpet of Conscience*, p. 68
(see BROTHERHOOD, WORLD PERSPECTIVE)

M

MAJORITY

Success, recognition, and conformity are the bywords of the modern world where everyone seems to crave the anesthetizing security of being identified with the majority.

—*The Strength to Love*, p. 8
(see LEADER, NONCONFORMISM, SUCCESS)

MALCOLM X

It has been said that Martin Luther King was the only man who could stop a riot just by saying a few words, and Malcolm X was the only man who could start one. Martin Luther King and Malcolm X met only once, on March 26, 1964, at the U.S. Capitol. On that occasion they both pledged their efforts to pressure Congress into passing the pending Civil Rights Bill.

They came to symbolize two opposite choices for black Americans toward achieving the goal of freedom. It was Dr. King's view that nonviolence was the only method that could succeed; it was Malcolm X's view that oppressed people had the right to use any means necessary, even violence. Both men respected each other's personal courage and leadership qualities, although Malcolm X was more openly critical of King than King was of Malcolm X.

Malcolm X paid a visit to Coretta King once in 1965 while King was in Selma Jail. Malcolm told Coretta he respected what Dr. King was trying to do and hoped King would succeed. In the meantime, he said, he would continue preaching his own, more militant, gospel. "Maybe white folks will listen more carefully to Dr. King if they know what the alternative is." Three weeks later, on February 21, 1965, Malcolm X was gunned down in Harlem by blacks allegedly associated with the Muslims.

(see X)

MAN

"My faith in man is, at bottom, a faith in God," King preached in a sermon on February 26, 1956. Man is a spiritual being made in the image of God, according to King. Man's spiritual nature is expressed in the human faculties of reason, memory, imagination, and freedom. Man's innate freedom is seen in free will and the ability "to deliberate, to make decisions and to choose between alternatives."

The universe is structured so that man ultimately determines his own destiny, although appearances may be to the contrary. With the faculties of memory and imagination, man is able to transcend the limits of nature, time, and space. Examples of this transcendent spiritual capacity include man's artistic achievements—the ability to create literature, to paint masterpieces, or to write stirring compositions of music.

The body is not evil. God created the body, and all that

God created is good. The idea that the body is evil has no place in Christianity, in King's view; it is derived from Greek philosophy. "Christianity, on the other hand, contends that the will, and not the body, is the principle of evil. The body is both sacred and significant in Christian thought."

According to King, the Christian doctrine is that evil lies in man's will. Evil comes from the misuse of free will. When man becomes evil it is because man, freely choosing between alternatives, chooses evil instead of good.

Man is neither innately good nor is he innately bad; he has potentialities for both.

—"Love, Law and Civil Disobedience,"
New South, vol. 16, December 1961, p. 6

Man is a being of spirit.... An abiding expression of man's spiritual nature is his freedom. Man is man because he is free to operate within the framework of his destiny. He is free to deliberate, to make decisions, and to choose between alternatives. He is distinguished from animals by his freedom to do evil or to do good and to walk the high road of beauty or tread the low road of ugly degeneracy.

—*The Strength to Love*, p. 90

The Renaissance was too optimistic, and the Reformation was too pessimistic. The former so concentrated on the goodness of man that it overlooked his capacity for evil; the latter so concentrated on the wickedness of man that it overlooked his capacity for goodness.

—*The Strength to Love*, p. 121
(see CHOICE, EVIL, GOD, HUMAN NATURE, SIN)

MANKIND

Every nation must now develop an overriding loyalty to mankind as a whole in order to preserve the best in their individual societies.

—Where Do We Go from Here? p. 190
(see LOYALTY, WORLD PERSPECTIVE)

MAN OF THE YEAR

King's cool, determined gaze appeared on the cover of *Time* magazine in its January 3, 1964 edition as its Man of the Year, only the second black man since Emperor Haile Selassie to receive that honor. "Few can explain the extraordinary King mystique," said the article, "yet he has an indescribable capacity for empathy that is the touchstone of leadership. By deed and by preachment, he has stirred in his people a Christian forbearance that nourishes hope and smothers injustice."

King was publically gracious, saying the honor was not a personal one. "I would like to think that my selection . . . was not a personal tribute, but a tribute to the whole freedom movement," he wrote in the SCLC newsletter.

In private, however, he was stung by the more critical portions of the *Time* article, which said he lacked the "quiet brilliance" of Roy Wilkins or the "bristling wit" of James Baldwin. What hurt the most was the criticism of his style of speech and his use of exaggerated metaphors. Segregation, he was quoted as saying, was "the adultery of an illicit intercourse between injustice and immorality" that could not be "cured by the vaseline of gradualism." Although *Time* criticized it, time has vindicated the eloquence of Martin Luther King.

(see DREAM)

MARCHING RHETORIC

No one could inspire a crowd of freedom marchers the way Martin Luther King could. When he spoke before a march he would fire up the crowd's enthusiasm. People in the audience would answer back after each line of his marching rhetoric. If you listen to a tape of his speech before the Selma march, it sounds like this:

I got on my marching shoes!

Yes, Lord, me too.

I woke up this morning with my mind stayed on freedom!

Preach, doctor, preach!

I ain't going to let nobody turn me around!

Let's march, brother; we are with you.

If the road to freedom leads through the jailhouse, then, turnkey, swing wide the gates!

Praise the Lord!

Some of you are afraid.

That's right; that's right.

Some of you are contented.

Speak, speak, speak!

But if you won't go, don't hinder me! We shall march nonviolently. We shall force this nation, this city, this world, to face its own conscience. We will make the God of love in the white man triumphant over the Satan of segregation that is in him. The struggle is not between black and white!

No, no!

But between good and evil.

That's it, that's it.

And whenever good and evil have a confrontation, good will win!

Praise the Lord!

(see SERMON)

On June 22, 1963, a group of civil rights leaders met with President Kennedy in the White House and announced to him their plan for a March on Washington to demonstrate for civil rights. Kennedy, who had just announced his proposed Civil Rights Bill, was afraid the demonstration might get out of control and hurt the bill's chances in Congress.

"The March," suggested Dr. King, "could serve as a means of dramatizing the issue and mobilizing support in parts of the country which don't know the problem at first hand."

"I think it may be ill-timed," said President Kennedy.

"Frankly, I have never engaged in any direct action movement which did not seem ill-timed," replied Dr. King, with just a hint of ironic humor. "Many people thought Birmingham ill-timed."

President Kennedy couldn't repress a grin, for he knew Dr. King was referring to him, among others. When JFK realized he couldn't dissuade the black leadership from holding the march, he agreed to support it.

The President's fears of a riot proved unfounded. The March on Washington was a peaceful triumph. A crowd estimated at 250,000, a third of them white, marched together to the Capitol. People of different races and religions linked arms in an unprecedented demonstration of unity. Many celebrities came to the podium. Burt Lancaster read a speech written by James Baldwin, with Marlon Brando, Charlton Heston, Sidney Poitier, Harry Belafonte, and others standing by. The first black Nobel prize winner, Ralph Bunche, was there, with Josephine Baker, Jackie Robinson, Lena Horne, and Sammy Davis, Jr., to name a few. But the climax of the event was Martin Luther King's soul-stirring speech with its ringing refrain: "I have a dream ..."

(see Biography 1963, DREAM)

MARTIN LUTHER KING, JR., DAY

Public Law 98-144, passed by the 98th Congress on November 2, 1983, established a national holiday in honor of Dr. King. He is the first black American so honored. The law reads as follows:

AN ACT

To amend title 5, United States Code, to make the birthday of Martin Luther King, Jr., a legal holiday.

Be it enacted by the Senate and House of Representatives of the United States of America in Congress assembled, That section 6103(a) of title 5, United States Code, is amended by inserting immediately below the item relating to New Year's Day the following:

"Birthday of Martin Luther King, Jr., the third Monday in January."

SEC. 2. The Amendment made by the first section of this Act shall take effect on the first January 1 that occurs after the two-year period following the date of the enactment of this Act.

Approved November 2, 1983
(see Biography 1986)

MASS MEDIA

The world seldom believes the horror stories of history until they are documented via the mass media.

—Letter to Harold Courlander, October 30, 1961
(see EXPOSURE, INJUSTICE)

MATERIALISM

Violence has been the inseparable twin of materialism, the hallmark of its grandeur and misery.

—*Where Do We Go from Here?* p. 66
(see ECONOMIC INJUSTICE, POVERTY)

MEANS

One of the great philosophical debates of history has been over the whole question of means and ends. And there have always been those who argued that the end justifies the means, that the means really aren't important. The important thing is to get to the end, you see.

So, if you're seeking to develop a just society, they say, the important thing is to get there, and the means aren't really important. Any means will do so long as you get there—they may be violent, they may be untruthful means; they may even be unjust means to a just end.

There have been those who have argued this throughout history. But we will never have peace in the world until men everywhere recognize that ends are not cut off from means, because the means represent the ideal in the making, and the end in process, and ultimately you can't reach good ends through evil means, because the means represent the seed and the end represents the tree.

—*The Trumpet of Conscience,* pp. 70–71

Means and ends must cohere because the end is pre-existent in the means, and ultimately destructive means cannot bring about constructive ends.

—*The Trumpet of Conscience,* p. 71

I have consistently preached that nonviolence demands that the means we use must be as pure as the ends we seek.

—Letter from Birmingham Jail, 1963

It is wrong to use immoral means to attain moral ends. . . . It is just as wrong, or perhaps even more so, to use moral means to preserve immoral ends.

—Letter from Birmingham Jail, 1963

There is always a danger that we will permit the means by which we live to replace the ends for which we live.

—*The Strength to Love*, p. 52

The means by which we live have outdistanced the ends for which we live. Our scientific power has outrun our spiritual power. We have guided missiles and misguided men.

—*The Strength to Love*, p. 57
(see ENDS)

MIDDLE-CLASS VALUES

"It is ironic that today so many educators and sociologists are seeking methods to instill middle-class values in Negro youth as the ideal in social development," observed King, who felt middle-class values were less important than human values. "It was precisely when young Negroes threw off their middle-class values that they made an historic contribution."

Middle-class values stress the importance of career and money. These were not the values which led to the civil rights movement; these are not the values which lead to positive social transformation. Looking back on the triumphs of the civil rights movement, King contended that the young blacks who made history in the early 1960s were those who were willing to put aside their middle-class ambitions and values, at least temporarily. "They abandoned those values when they put careers and wealth in a secondary role. When they cheerfully became jailbirds and troublemakers, when they took off their Brooks Brothers attire and put on overalls to work in the isolated rural south, they challenged and inspired white youth to emulate them."

(see CIVIL DISOBEDIENCE, STUDENTS, YOUTH)

MILITARY DEFENSE

A nation that continues year after year to spend more money on military defense than on programs of social uplift is approaching spiritual doom.

—The Trumpet of Conscience, p. 33
(see PEACE, VIETNAM WAR, WAR)

MINORITIES

The hope of the world is still in dedicated minorities. The trailblazers in human, academic, and religious freedom have always been in the minority.

—Where Do We Go from Here? p. 95

I'm interested in rights for Negroes, but I'm just as interested in Appalachian whites and Mexican-Americans and other minorities.

—Press conference, Cleveland, April 26, 1967
(see BROTHERHOOD, HUMAN BEINGS,
LOYALTY, WORLD PERSPECTIVE)

MODERATES

By the time of the Birmingham campaign in 1963, King had become discouraged with the lack of support from those moderates who disapproved of racism but also seemed to disapprove of taking any steps to eradicate it.

"I must confess that over the last few years I have been gravely disappointed by the white moderate," he wrote in his Letter from Birmingham Jail. "I have almost reached the regrettable conclusion that the Negro's great stumblingblock is not the White Citizen's Council-er or the Ku Klux Klanner, but the white moderate who is more devoted to 'order' than to justice, who prefers a negative peace which is the absence of tension to a positive peace which is the presence of justice, who constantly says 'I agree with you in the goal you seek, but I can't agree with your methods of direct action,' who paternalistically believes that he can set the timetable for another man's freedom."

(see LAW AND ORDER, PEACE, TENSION)

MONEY

After the Watts riots had devastated the black ghetto of Los Angeles, King visited the riot-torn area. The desolation he saw there made a deep impression on him.

"I'll never forget the discussion we had with King that night," recollected Bayard Rustin. "He was absolutely undone, and he looked at me and said, 'You know, Bayard, I worked to get these people the right to eat hamburgers, and now I've got to do something . . . to help them get the money to buy it.'"

Jesus never made a sweeping statement against wealth. Rather, he condemned the misuse of wealth. Money, like any other force such as electricity, is amoral and can be used for either good or evil.

—*The Strength to Love*, p. 51
(see also GODS, GUARANTEED NATIONAL INCOME, POVERTY)

MONTGOMERY BUS BOYCOTT

It began with the arrest of Rosa Parks for refusing to give up her seat to a white man on a public bus. "That was the day that we started a bus protest which literally electrified the nation," recounted King. "And that was the day when we decided that we were not going to take segregated buses any longer. And, you know, when we planned the bus boycott we said if we could just get about fifty or sixty percent of the Negroes of Montgomery not to ride buses this would be an effective boycott. I think that whole day we found eight Negroes on the buses. And from that day on that boycott was more than ninety-nine and nine-tenths effective."

The Montgomery Improvement Association was formed and Martin Luther King was surprised to find himself nominated its president and spokesperson. "The action caught me unawares. It happened so quickly that I did not even have time to think it through." Although he was well qualified to be a leader, he did not know that he had been chosen for other reasons; because he was new to Montgomery he had fewer enemies and was less entrenched in the community. The others felt that it would be easier for King to pack up and leave town, if necessary, than it would for those with longer roots in Montgomery.

Three hours after his surprising election as leader of the boycott, King gave a sermon to four thousand people at the Holt Street Church. After cataloging the injustices of the bus company, to a chorus of "Amens" he proclaimed the words that signaled the beginning of a new age of civil rights activism:

"But there comes a time when people get tired. We are here this evening to say to those who have mistreated us so long that we are tired—tired of being segregated and humiliated, tired of being kicked about by the brutal feet of oppression. We have no alternative but to protest.

"For many years, we have shown amazing patience. We have sometimes given our white brothers the feeling that we liked the way we were being treated. But we come here tonight to be saved from that patience that makes us patient with anything less than freedom and justice."

It was a long struggle. King was arrested; his house was bombed; he and his family received numerous death threats. But in the end the boycott was successful. It brought an end to the system of segregation on public buses in Montgomery.

It ended with the Supreme Court ruling on November 13, 1956, that "affirmed a decision of a special three-judge U.S. District Court in declaring Alabama's state and local laws requiring segregation on buses unconstitutional."

On the evening of December 20, 1956, Dr. King called off the strike and urged the black citizens of Montgomery "to return to the buses on a desegregated basis." At 5:55 a.m. the next morning, TV cameras recorded the moment for posterity as Dr. King was the first to get on a bus. He was accompanied by Ralph Abernathy, Ed Nixon, and Glenn Smiley, other leaders of the boycott.

As King boarded the bus, the driver recognized him. "Is that you, Dr. King?" asked the white driver. King nodded. The driver tipped his hat. "Glad to have you with us this morning."

This is not a drama with only one actor . . . It is the chronicle of 50,000 Negroes who took to heart the principles of nonviolence, who learned to fight for their rights with the weapon of love, and who, in the process, acquired a new estimate of their own human worth.

—Preface, *Stride Toward Freedom*, 1958
(see Biography 1955–56, BOMBING, CUSTOM, NEGATIVE PEACE, RECONCILIATION, WALKING)

MORALITY

If there is to be peace on earth and good will toward men, we must finally believe in the ultimate morality of the universe, and believe that all reality hinges on moral foundations.

—*The Trumpet of Conscience*, p. 75
(see GOD, HISTORY, UNIVERSE)

MORAL RELATIVISM

Moral principles have lost their distinctiveness. For modern man, absolute right and absolute wrong are a matter of what the majority is doing. Right and wrong are relative to likes and dislikes and the customs of a particular community. We have unconsciously applied Einstein's theory of relativity, which properly described the physical universe, to the moral and ethical realm.

—*The Strength to Love*, p. 43

MOTIVE

I have come to see even more that as we move on toward the goal of justice, hatred must *never* be our motive.

—Speech, Chicago, August 24, 1963
(see ENDS, HATRED, JUSTICE, MEANS)

MURDER

On August 4, 1964, the bodies of three civil rights workers—James Chaney, Michael Schwerner, and Andrew

Goodman—were found in a shallow grave outside Philadelphia, Mississippi. They had been murdered shortly after being released from a Philadelphia jail. Two years later, the murderers were still free.

On the anniversary of the murder, King led a small march through Philadelphia. While a crowd of hostile whites gathered, King conducted a brief memorial service for the murdered victims. At one point Deputy Sheriff Cecil Ray Price tried to block his path. King looked him squarely in the eye.

"You're the one who had Schwerner and those fellows in jail?" asked King. "Yes, sir," answered Price proudly. By now the crowd of whites numbered more than three hundred. "I believe in my heart that the murderers are somewhere around me at this moment," declared Dr. King to his followers. "You're damn right, they're right behind you now," said Price.

King later recalled this as one of the most frightening moments in his long career. "I had yielded to the real possibility of the inevitability of death."

After the memorial was over, King led his followers back to a church, where he told reporters, "This is a terrible town; the worst city I have ever seen. There is a complete reign of terror here."

Ultimately Deputy Price and six others in Philadelphia were found guilty of the murders, but not before King had written his last book, *Where Do We Go from Here: Chaos or Community?* expressing outrage about the many unprosecuted murders in Mississippi: "In Mississippi the murder of civil rights workers is still a popular pastime. In that state more than forty Negroes and whites have either been lynched or murdered over the past three years, and not a single man has been punished for these crimes."

N

NATIVE AMERICANS

The history of racism in America did not begin with the African Americans, according to Dr. King. It began with the Native American Indians. "Our nation was born in genocide when it embraced the doctrine that the original American, the Indian, was an inferior race," he wrote in *Why We Can't Wait*. "Even before there were large numbers of Negroes on our shores, the scar of racial hatred had already disfigured colonial society."

(see AMERICA, RACISM)

NEGATIVE FREEDOM

There is such a thing as the freedom of exhaustion. Some people are so worn down by the yoke of oppression that they give up. A few years ago in the slum areas of Atlanta, a Negro guitarist used to sing almost daily: "Been down so long that down don't bother me." This is the type of negative freedom and resignation that often engulfs the life of the oppressed.

—*Stride Toward Freedom*, p. 212
(see APATHY, GOD, HOPE)

NEGATIVE PEACE

During the Montgomery Bus Boycott one of the leading white citizens approached King after a council meeting and said, "Over the years we have had such peaceful and harmonious race relations here. Why must you and your associates destroy this long tradition?"

"Sir, you have never had a real peace in Montgomery," King replied. "You have had a sort of negative peace in which the Negro too often accepted his state of subordination. But this is not true peace. True peace is not merely the absence of tension; it is the presence of justice. The tension we see in Montgomery today is the necessary tension that comes when the oppressed rise up and start to move forward toward a permanent, positive peace."

(see CRISIS, CUSTOM, EXPOSURE, INJUSTICE, PEACE, TENSION)

NEIGHBORLINESS

One of the great tragedies of man's long trek along the highway of history has been the limiting of neighborly concern to tribe, race, class, or nation.

—*The Strength to Love*, p. 17
(see LOYALTY, WORLD PERSPECTIVE)

NEW WORLD ORDER

It is historically and biologically true that there can be no birth and growth without birth and growing pains. Whenever there is the emergence of the new we confront the recalcitrance of the old. So the tensions which we witness in the world today are indicative of the fact that a new world order is being born and an old order is passing away.

—Address, First Annual Institute on
Nonviolence and Social Change,
Montgomery, Alabama, December 3, 1956
(see AMERICAN REVOLUTION, BACKLASH,
REVOLUTION, WORLD REVOLUTION)

NEW YORK NIGHTCAP

King did not drink spirits regularly, but he did take a drink socially on occasion. It was Julie Belafonte, the wife of performer Harry Belafonte, who introduced Martin to Harvey's Bristol Cream. For years he kept up a running gag with the Belafontes about how much he relished the "nightcap of the most elegant New Yorkers."

The Belafontes gave him a bottle of Harvey's Bristol Cream as a gift, but he preferred to keep it at their home and drink it only when in their company. Every time King visited the Belafontes he would make a big show of inspecting the bottle to determine whether the sherry had slipped below the line that he had carefully marked at the end of his last visit.

"Has the devil been drinking my sherry?" he wanted to know. "Every time I come to New York I get the feeling the devil's been here first."

(see HUMOR, ICE CREAM)

NIXON, RICHARD

"Nixon has a genius for convincing one that he is sincere." This was King's cool assessment after meeting Vice President Nixon in 1959. "He almost disarms you with his sincerity." King added: "If Richard Nixon is not sincere, he is the most dangerous man in America."

(see EISENHOWER, JOHNSON, KENNEDY, JOHN F.)

At age thirty-five, Martin Luther King was the youngest man ever to receive the Nobel Peace Prize. He was in a hospital in Atlanta recovering from exhaustion when his wife woke him up with the news.

"How is the Nobel Peace Prize winner for 1964 feeling this morning?"

King was still groggy. "What's that?"

"The Associated Press just called. The announcement has just been made and you are the winner."

King wondered if he was still dreaming.

"We had quite a time getting him ready," was Coretta King's recollection of the hectic hours preceding the ceremony on December 11, 1964, as King was dressed up in a frock coat, striped cravat, and pin-stripe trousers. The ascot gave him the most trouble. "Martin kept fussing and making funny comments about having to wear such a ridiculous thing." He swore he would never again "gird" himself in such "garb."

The presentation took place in Oslo University's auditorium, attended by King Olav V and Crown Prince Harald of Norway, among other dignitaries. A small contingent of Martin's friends and family members, including his father and wife, were also on hand to see his triumph.

The chairman of the Norwegian Parliament's Nobel Committee introduced Martin Luther King as a "champion of peace," hailing him as the "first person in the western world to have shown us that a struggle can be waged without violence."

King rose to thunderous applause. He accepted the prize, a gold medal and the scroll Dr. Gunnar Jahn presented him. Swallowing nervously, he began: "Your Majesty, Your Royal Highness, Mr. President, Excellencies, ladies and gentlemen, I accept the Nobel Prize for Peace at a moment when twenty-two million Negroes of the

United States of America are engaged in a creative battle to end the long night of racial injustice."

King accepted the award not for himself alone, he said, but on behalf of the civil rights movement. He felt the award was being given to him as the "trustee" of a movement that offered a definitive answer to the world's need for social change: nonviolence.

"I am mindful that only yesterday in Birmingham, Alabama, our children, crying out for brotherhood, were answered with fire hoses, snarling dogs, and even death.

"I am mindful that only yesterday in Philadelphia, Mississippi, young people seeking to secure the right to vote were brutalized and murdered.

"Therefore I must ask why this prize is awarded to a movement which is beleaguered and committed to an unrelenting struggle, to a movement which has not won the very peace and brotherhood which is the essence of the Nobel Prize.

"After contemplation I conclude that this award, which I receive on behalf of the movement, is a profound recognition that nonviolence is the answer to the crucial political and racial questions of our time—the need for man to overcome oppression without resorting to violence.

"Man must evolve for all human conflict a method which rejects revenge, aggression and retaliation. The foundation of such a method is love.

"I accept this award today with an abiding faith in America and an audacious faith in mankind. I refuse to accept the idea that man is mere flotsam and jetsam in the river of life which surrounds him. I refuse to accept the view that mankind is so tragically bound to the starless midnight of racism and war that the bright daylight of peace can never become a reality.

"I believe that unarmed truth and unconditional love will have the final word in reality," he declared.

He concluded with a tribute to the millions on whose

behalf he had traveled to Oslo, millions whose names would never be found in *Who's Who*.

"Yet when the years have rolled past and when the blazing light of truth is focussed on this marvelous age in which we live—men and women will know and children will be taught that we have a finer land, a better people, a more noble civilization—because these humble children of God were willing to suffer for righteousness' sake."

The audience gave Martin Luther King, Jr., a standing ovation. Congratulations came pouring in from all over the world. "This is a tribute to the leadership you have given to the movement for individual dignity and equality of opportunity," said a message from President Johnson.

The Nobel Peace Prize was a great honor, but it was also a great responsibility. It raised Dr. King to the stature of the international leader of the peace movement—an international spokesman. He could no longer simply be a spokesman for blacks, or for civil rights. The world had recognized him as its principal spokesman for peace. The world looked to Martin Luther King for wisdom and guidance in mankind's neverending quest.

"I cannot forget that the Nobel Prize for Peace was also a commission—a commission to work harder than I had ever worked before for 'the brotherhood of man.' This is a calling which takes me beyond national allegiances."

The $50,000 prize was divided, at Dr. King's request, among the major civil rights organizations, including the Southern Christian Leadership Conference.

(see NONVIOLENCE, PEACE, PRIZE WINNER)

NONCONFORMISM

We as Christians have a mandate to be nonconformists.

—*The Strength to Love*, p. 8

This hour in history needs a dedicated circle of transformed nonconformists. Our planet teeters on the brink of atomic annihilation; dangerous passions of pride, hatred, and self-ishness are enthroned in our lives; truth lies prostrate on the rugged hills of nameless cavalries; and men do reverence before the false gods of nationalism and materialism.

—*The Strength to Love*, p. 13
(see CONFORMISM, GODS, LEADER, MAJORITY)

NONCOOPERATION

Noncooperation with evil was the moral basis of the Montgomery Bus Boycott, as King conceived it. "In order to be true to one's conscience and true to God, a righteous man has no alternative but to refuse to cooperate with an evil system," he wrote in *Stride Toward Freedom*. "From this moment on I conceived of our movement as an act of massive noncooperation. From then on I rarely used the word 'boycott.' "

Noncooperation with evil is as much a moral obligation as is cooperation with good.

—*Stride Toward Freedom*, p. 212
(see EVIL, GANDHI, NONVIOLENT RESISTANCE)

NONVIOLENCE

Nonviolence does not mean refusing to fight. Nonviolence is a way of fighting without resorting to violence. It is a method of fighting for what you believe in, without giving in to oppression and without oppressing others. It is a way of winning a lasting victory instead of a temporary advantage. It is a way of ending the conflict by refusing to perpetuate it. It is a way of overcoming evil by refusing to play the game according to evil's rules.

Nonviolence was Dr. King's method of fighting. "I've

decided that I'm going to do battle for my philosophy," he declared. "I can't make myself believe that God wants me to hate. I'm tired of violence. And I'm not going to let my oppressor dictate to me what method I must use."

He chose nonviolence, following in the footsteps of Christ and Gandhi before him. "The beauty of nonviolence," he explained, "is that it seeks to break the chain reaction of evil." One of his most eloquent expressions of the nonviolent philosophy was made in his Christmas Eve sermon of 1967:

I've seen too much hate to want to hate, myself, and I've seen hate on the faces of too many sheriffs, too many White Citizens Councilors, and too many Klansmen of the South to want to hate, myself; and every time I see it, I say to myself, hate is too great a burden to bear.

Somehow we must be able to stand up before our most bitter opponents and say: "We shall match your capacity to inflict suffering by our capacity to endure suffering. We will meet your physical force with soul force. Do to us what you will and we will still love you.

"We cannot in all good conscience obey your unjust laws and abide by the unjust system, because noncooperation with evil is as much a moral obligation as is cooperation with good, and so throw us in jail and we will still love you.

"Bomb our homes and threaten our children, and, as difficult as it is, we will still love you. Send your hooded perpetrators of violence into our communities at the midnight hour and drag us out on some wayside road and leave us half-dead as you beat us, and we will still love you.

"Send your propaganda agents around the country and make it appear that we are not fit, culturally and otherwise, for integration, but we'll still love you.

"But be assured that we'll wear you down by our capacity to suffer, and one day we will win our freedom. We will not only win freedom for ourselves, we will so appeal to your heart and conscience that we will win you in the process, and our victory will be a double victory."

* * *

Nonviolent resistance had emerged as the technique of the movement, while love stood as the regulating ideal. In other words, Christ furnished the spirit and motivation, while Gandhi furnished the method.

—*Stride Toward Freedom*, p. 85

We are a nation that worships the frontier tradition, and our heroes are those who champion justice through violent retaliation against injustice. It is not simple to adopt a credo that moral force has as much strength and virtue as the capacity to return a physical blow; or that to refrain from hitting back requires more will and bravery than the automatic reflexes of defense.

—*Why We Can't Wait*, p. 37

It is my hope that as the Negro plunges deeper into the quest for freedom and justice he will plunge even deeper into the philosophy of nonviolence. The Negro all over the South must come to the point that he can say to his white brother: "We will match your capacity to inflict suffering with our capacity to endure suffering. We will meet your physical force with soul force. We will not hate you, but we will obey your evil laws. We will soon wear you down by pure capacity to suffer."

—Letter to Chester Bowles (former Ambassador to India), October 18, 1957

Nonviolence ... does not seek to defeat or humiliate the opponent, but to win his friendship and understanding.

—*Stride Toward Freedom*, p. 102

The nonviolent approach does not immediately change the heart of the oppressor. It first does something to the hearts and souls of those committed to it. It gives them new self-respect; it calls up resources of strength and courage that they did not know they had. Finally it reaches the opponent and so stirs his conscience that reconciliation becomes a reality.

—*Stride Toward Freedom*, p. 219

Nonviolence is a powerful and just weapon. It is a weapon unique in history, which cuts without wounding, and ennobles the man who wields it. It is a sword that heals.

—*Why We Can't Wait*, p. 26

Nonviolence in the truest sense is not a strategy that one uses simply because it is expedient at the moment; nonviolence is ultimately a way of life that men live by because of the sheer morality of its claim. But even granting this, the willingness to use nonviolence as a technique is a step forward. For he who goes this far is more likely to adopt nonviolence later as a way of life.

—*Stride Toward Freedom*, p. 89

We have experimented with the meaning of nonviolence in our struggle for racial justice in the United States, but now the time has come for man to experiment with nonviolence in all areas of human conflict, and that means nonviolence on an international scale.

—*The Trumpet of Conscience*, p. 68

The aftermath of nonviolence is the creation of the beloved community, while the aftermath of violence is tragic bitterness.

—*Stride Toward Freedom*, p. 102

Today, the choice is no longer between violence and nonviolence. It is either nonviolence or nonexistence.

—*Stride Toward Freedom*, p. 224
(see also CHRISTIAN LOVE, GANDHI,
LOVE, NONVIOLENT RESISTANCE)

NONVIOLENT RESISTANCE

"Tested in Montgomery during the winter of 1955–56, and toughened throughout the South in the eight ensuing years," wrote King in *Why We Can't Wait,* "nonviolent resistance had become, by 1963, the logical force in the greatest mass action crusade for freedom that has ever occurred in American history."

Nonviolent resistance does not aim to humiliate or defeat opponents but to liberate them from their fears and prejudices. The purpose is always liberation, never humiliation.

Nonviolent resistance against the white oppressors is what Dr. King urged his people to practice in the segregated South of the 1950s and 1960s. He was able to point to a few important precedents for this revolutionary method, suggesting that it is part of the most important movement in history.

"The religious tradition of the Negro had shown him that the nonviolent resistance of the early Christians had constituted a moral offensive of such overriding power that it shook the Roman empire. American history had taught him that nonviolence in the form of boycotts and protests had confounded the British monarchy and laid the basis for freeing the colonies from unjust domination. Within his own century, the nonviolent ethic of Mahatma Gandhi and his followers had muzzled the guns of the British empire in India and freed more than three hundred and fifty million people from colonialism."

* * *

The principle of nonviolent resistance seeks to reconcile the truths of two opposites—acquiescence and violence—while avoiding the extremes and immoralities of both. The nonviolent resister agrees with the person who acquiesces that one should not be physically aggressive toward his opponent; but he balances the equation by agreeing with the person of violence that evil must be resisted. He avoids the nonresistance of the former and the violent resistance of the latter.

—*Stride Toward Freedom*, p. 213

Nonviolent resistance is not a method for cowards; it does resist. If one uses this method because he is afraid or merely because he lacks the instruments of violence, he is not truly nonviolent.

—*Stride Toward Freedom*, p. 102

The nonviolent resister must often express his protest through noncooperation or boycotts, but he realizes these are not ends in themselves; they are merely means to awaken a sense of moral shame in the opponent. The end is redemption and reconciliation.

—*Stride Toward Freedom*, p. 102

Nonviolent resistance is not aimed against oppressors but against oppression. Under its banner consciences, not racial groups, are enlisted.

—*Stride Toward Freedom*, p. 214

Its opponents are revealed as the instigators and practitioners of violence if it occurs. Then public support is magnetically attracted to the advocates of nonviolence, while those who employ violence are literally disarmed by overwhelming sentiment against their stand.

—*Stride Toward Freedom*, p. 215

Nonviolent resistance ... is based on the conviction that the universe is on the side of justice.... The believer in nonviolence has deep faith in the future.... For he knows that in his struggle for justice he has cosmic companionship.

—*Stride Toward Freedom*, p. 106

The nonviolent resister not only refuses to shoot his opponent but he also refuses to hate him. At the center of nonviolence stands the principle of love.

—*Stride Toward Freedom*, pp. 102–3
(see GANDHI, LOVE, NONVIOLENCE, SYNTHESIS)

NOW

Now is the time to make real the promise of democracy and transform our pending national elegy into a creative psalm of brotherhood.

—Letter from Birmingham Jail, 1963

OPPRESSION

Oppressed people cannot remain oppressed forever. The yearning for freedom eventually manifests itself, and this is what has happened with the American Negro. Something within has reminded him of his birthright of freedom, and something without has reminded him that it can be gained.

—Nobel address, December 11, 1964

Often the oppressor goes along unaware of the evil involved in his oppression so long as the oppressed accepts it.

—*Stride Toward Freedom*, p. 51
(see EVIL, FREEDOM, NONCOOPERATION, WORLD REVOLUTION)

ORGANIZATION

To produce change, people must be organized to work together in units of power.

—*Where Do We Go from Here?* p. 131
(see CIVIL RIGHTS, POWER)

OTHERS

From time immemorial men have lived by the principle that "self-preservation is the first law of life." But this is a false assumption. I would say that other-preservation is the first law of life. It is the first law of life precisely because we cannot preserve self without being concerned about preserving other selves.

—*Where Do We Go from Here?* p. 180
(see GREATNESS, SERVICE)

P

PACIFISM

True pacifism is not unrealistic submission to an evil power.... It is rather a courageous confrontation with evil by the power of love, in the faith that it is better to be the recipient of violence than the inflicter of it, since the latter only multiplies the existence of violence and bitterness in the universe, while the former may develop a sense of shame in the opponent, and thereby bring about a transformation and change of heart.

—*Stride Toward Freedom*, pp. 98–99
(see LOVE, NONVIOLENCE)

PASSIVE RESISTANCE

The phrase "passive resistance" often gives the false impression that this is a sort of "do-nothing method" in which the resister quietly and passively accepts evil. But nothing is further from the truth. For while the nonviolent resister is passive in the sense that he is not physically aggressive toward his opponent, his mind and emotions are always active, constantly seeking to persuade his opponent that he is wrong. The method is passive physically, but strongly active spiritually. It is not passive nonresistance to evil, it is active nonviolent resistance to evil.

—*Stride Toward Freedom,* p. 102
(see ACTIVISM, NONVIOLENCE, NONVIOLENT RESISTANCE)

PEACE

"It is one of the strangest things that all the great military geniuses of the world have talked about peace," mused Martin Luther King in his last Christmas Eve sermon on December 24, 1967. "The conquerors of old who came killing in pursuit of peace—Alexander, Julius Caesar, Charlemagne, and Napoleon—were akin in seeking a peaceful world order. If you will read *Mein Kampf* closely enough, you will discover that Hitler contended that everything he did in Germany was for peace. And the leaders of the world today talk eloquently about peace.

"Every time we drop our bombs in North Vietnam, President Johnson talks eloquently about peace. What is the problem? They are talking about peace as a distant goal, as an end we seek, but one day we must come to see that peace is not merely a distant goal we seek, but that it is a means by which we arrive at that goal. We must pursue peaceful ends through peaceful means."

One of the most persistent ambiguities we face is that everybody talks about peace as a goal, but among the wielders of power peace is practically nobody's business. Many men cry "Peace! Peace!" but they refuse to do the things that make for peace.

—*Where Do We Go from Here?* p. 182

True peace is not merely the absence of tension, but it is the presence of justice.

—Speech, "True Peace," Atlanta, July 5, 1962
(see ARMS RACE, ENDS, JUSTICE, MEANS, WAR)

PERSONALITY

Martin Luther King placed high value on the human personality, for he regarded personality as a reflection of the soul and therefore an image of the divine. The personality is not only an expression of the soul's individuality; it is a unique image of God, one of the many images created by God to reflect the infinite in the finite. Because every personality is divine in essence, every personality is endowed with dignity and worth.

"Deeply rooted in our political and religious heritage is the conviction that every man is an heir to a legacy of dignity and worth," King wrote in an article titled "The Ethical Demands of Integration." "This innate worth referred to in the phrase *image of God* is universally shared in equal portion by all men."

There must be a recognition of the sacredness of human personality.

—"The Ethical Demands of Integration,"
Religion and Labor, May 1963, p. 4

You can never see the *me* that makes me me, and I can never see the *you* that makes you you. That invisible something we call personality is beyond our physical gaze. Plato was right when he said that the visible is a shadow cast by the invisible.

—*The Strength to Love*, p. 75

To believe that human personality is the result of the fortuitous interplay of atoms and electrons is as absurd as to believe that a monkey by hitting typewriter keys at random will eventually produce a Shakespearean play.

—*The Strength to Love*, p. 55

Every human being has etched in his personality the indelible stamp of the Creator.

—*Where Do We Go from Here?* p. 97
(see GOD, HUMAN WORTH, IMAGE OF GOD, JUDEO-CHRISTIAN HERITAGE)

PHILOSOPHY

As a freshman at Morehouse College in 1944, young Martin Luther King, Jr., age fifteen, took his first introductory philosophy course, Philosophy 361, and received a grade of C. It was a discouraging start to his collegiate career. No one would have guessed that twenty years later King would establish himself as one of the world's greatest practical philosophers and be awarded the Nobel Peace Prize.

"He came to Morehouse rather young," testified Professor Williams, who taught the course that was required of all freshmen, "and it is not always the case that a student comes to full flower so young. So I would not say that he was the most outstanding student we had, for he was not."

It was during Professor Williams' course, however, that young MLK read Thoreau's essay *On Civil Disobedience*, which proved more seminal to his thinking than anything else he read until he discovered Gandhi's works in 1948.

(see Biography 1948, CIVIL DISOBEDIENCE, GANDHI)

PLEASURE

We have worshipped the god of pleasure only to discover that thrills play out and sensations are short-lived.

—*The Strength to Love*, p. 107
(see GODS)

PLEDGE

All volunteers for the sit-in demonstrations to protest segregated eating facilities in Birmingham, Alabama, 1963, were required to sign the following pledge. Similar pledges were used by Dr. King in other campaigns to register the commitment of his soldiers to nonviolence.

I HEREBY PLEDGE MYSELF—MY PERSON AND BODY—TO THE NONVIOLENT MOVEMENT. THEREFORE I WILL KEEP THE FOLLOWING TEN COMMANDMENTS.

1. MEDITATE daily on the teachings and life of Jesus.
2. REMEMBER always that the nonviolent in Birmingham seek justice and reconciliation—not victory.
3. WALK and TALK in the manner of love, for God is love.
4. PRAY daily to be used by God in order that all men might be free.
5. SACRIFICE personal wishes in order that all men might be free.
6. OBSERVE with both friend and foe the ordinary rules of courtesy.
7. SEEK to perform regular service for others and for the world.
8. REFRAIN from the violence of fist, tongue, or heart.
9. STRIVE to be in good spiritual and bodily health.
10. FOLLOW the directions of the movement and of the captain on a demonstration.

I sign this pledge, having seriously considered what I do and with the determination and will to persevere.

Name_____

Address_____

Phone_____

Nearest Relative_____

Address_____

Besides demonstrations, I could also help the movement by: (Circle the proper items)

Run errands, Drive my car, Fix food for volunteers, Clerical Work, Make phone calls, Answer phones, Mimeograph, Type, Print signs, Distribute leaflets.

ALABAMA CHRISTIAN MOVEMENT FOR HUMAN RIGHTS
BIRMINGHAM Affiliate of S.C.L.C.
505½ North 17th Street

(see CIVIL DISOBEDIENCE)

POOL

When Reverend Martin Luther King, Sr., came to visit his son at Crozer Seminary, he was shocked to see that his brilliant son dared to smoke cigarettes, drink beer, and play pool in his presence. "Would you like to play a game?" offered Martin, Jr., after guiding his father into the poolroom beneath the chapel.

The elder King gruffly refused. He folded his arms disapprovingly. But the younger King, who prided himself on his skill as a pool player, would not deny himself the pleasure. Defiantly, he began shooting pool while his father watched.

The father and son renewed their never-ending argument. The father said a pool hall was a place of sin, unbecoming to a man of God.

"Didn't Christ go out among the sinners?"

"To preach to them. Not to join them."

"It is not the smoke-filled pool hall that is sinful," said the son, "but the plan that is sometimes concocted here to rob the liquor store."

"And if more preachers played pool there would be fewer liquor stores robbed?" scoffed the father, shaking his head.

"If the sin was in the pool hall, we could eliminate the sin by eliminating the pool hall!" laughed the son, sinking a shot. "Do you believe that if there were fewer pool halls there would be fewer liquor stores robbed?"

"A pool hall is a place of temptation. 'Lead us not into temptation.' Matthew six."

" 'Are ye so without understanding? Do ye not perceive that whatsoever thing from without entereth into the man, it cannot defile him?' " replied the young divinity student, returning a short quote with a longer one. " 'All these evil things come from within and defile the man.' Mark, twenty-three. Evil comes from within."

"I can see I can't compete with you when it comes to quoting the Bible," snorted Daddy King. "Let me just remind you that the devil can cite chapter and verse when it suits his purpose."

"I'm not the devil, Dad," replied the future civil rights leader. "I'm your son. I've learned a great deal from you. Someday maybe you'll learn something from me."

(see POOL HALLS, VIETNAM WAR)

179

POOL HALLS

King's pool skills proved useful later, when he circulated the pool halls of Albany, Georgia, and Birmingham, Alabama, to preach nonviolence. After bottle-throwers disrupted a protest demonstration in Albany in the summer of 1962, King went to the pool hall to spread his gospel.

"I hate to hold up your pool game," he said, loosening his tie and picking up a pool cue. "I used to be a pool shark myself." He took a few shots and shook his head. "My skills have atrophied," he sighed, provoking sympathetic laughter.

Then he turned serious. King told the gathered pool hall patrons that the bottle-throwing and other acts of violence only played into the hands of the segregationists. "When you are violent," he said, "it makes them happy."

Similar problems occurred in Birmingham in 1963, when white violence provoked retaliation from some blacks. King went to the pool halls again and preached nonviolence. "When you are violent, the Ku Klux Klanners are happy," he said. "When you are violent, Bull Connor is happy."

(see RETALIATION)

POOR PEOPLE

The only real revolutionary, people say, is a man who has nothing to lose. There are millions of poor people in this country who have very little, or even nothing, to lose.

—*The Trumpet of Conscience*, p. 60

Economic security, decent sanitary housing, and quality education for every American.

—Statement of overall objectives, Poor People's Campaign, 1968
(see BILL OF RIGHTS FOR THE DISADVANTAGED,
GUARANTEED NATIONAL INCOME, POVERTY, THIRD WORLD)

POVERTY

"As long as there is poverty in the world I can never be rich," King liked to say, "even if I have a billion dollars." In the final years of his life, King came to consider poverty to be "mankind's second great evil," after racism.

Poverty is a form of violence, he insisted. It is an oppression against the human spirit. It is an injustice against the innate worth of every human being. It is a result of inequality rather than a proof of inequality.

King believed that the United States, as a nation, possessed sufficient wealth and resources to eliminate poverty. He argued that the existence of poverty in the United States should not be accepted as a necessary evil or an insoluble problem, but should be considered a national crisis requiring emergency measures. It is a matter of national will and national priorities, he said, not a matter of national resources.

The time has come for us to civilize ourselves by the total, direct and immediate abolition of poverty.

—*Where Do We Go from Here?* p. 164

We are demanding an emergency program to provide employment for everyone in need of a job or, if a work program is impracticable, a guaranteed annual income at levels that sustain life in decent circumstances. It is now incontestable that the wealth and resources of the United States make the elimination of poverty perfectly practical.

—*The Trumpet of Conscience*, p. 14

The dispossessed of this nation—the poor, both white and Negro—live in a cruelly unjust society. They must organize a revolution against that injustice, not against the lives of the persons who are their fellow citizens, but against the structures through which the society is refusing to take means which have been called for, and which are at hand, to lift the load of poverty.

—*The Trumpet of Conscience*, pp. 59–60

For the 35 million poor people in America—not even to mention, just yet, the poor in other nations—there is a kind of strangulation in the air. In our society it is murder, psychologically, to deprive a man of a job or an income. You are in substance saying to that man that he has no right to exist.

—*The Trumpet of Conscience*, p. 55

It is not only poverty that torments the Negro; it is the fact of poverty amid plenty. It is a misery generated by the gulf between the affluence he sees in the mass media and the deprivation he experiences in his everyday life.

—*Where Do We Go from Here?* p. 112

We are likely to find that the problems of housing and education, instead of preceding from the elimination of poverty, will themselves be affected if poverty is first abolished.

—*Where Do We Go from Here?* p. 164

There is nothing new about poverty. What is new, however, is that we now have the resources to get rid of it.

—*Where Do We Go from Here?* p. 177
(see BILL OF RIGHTS FOR THE DISADVANTAGED, GUARANTEED NATIONAL INCOME)

POWER

Power, properly understood, is the ability to achieve purpose. It is the strength required to bring about social, political, or economic changes. In this sense power is not only desirable but necessary in order to implement the demands of love and justice.

—*Where Do We Go from Here?* p. 37

One of the greatest problems of history is that the concepts of love and power are usually contrasted as polar opposites. Love is identified with a resignation of power and power with a denial of love ... What is needed is a realization that power without love is reckless and abusive and that love without power is sentimental and anemic. Power at its best is love implementing the demands of justice.

—*Where Do We Go from Here?* p. 37

There is nothing wrong with power. The problem is that in America power is unequally distributed.

—*Where Do We Go from Here?* p. 37

I'm not interested in power for power's sake, but I'm interested in power that is moral, that is right and that is good.

—Speech, Yazoo City, Mississippi, June 26, 1966

Power and morality must go together, implementing, fulfilling and ennobling each other. . . . Power at its best is the right use of strength.

—*Where Do We Go from Here?* p. 59
(see BLACK POWER, LOVE, MORALITY, ORGANIZATION)

PRAYER

During the Montgomery Bus Boycott there were many threats against King's life. Early one morning, after being awakened by such a call, he was unable to fall back asleep. Discouraged and exhausted, he climbed out of bed, shuffled into the kitchen, and made himself a cup of coffee. He began thinking of how he could remove himself from leadership in the boycott without appearing to be a coward.

He sat down at the kitchen table, staring at the cup of coffee. He folded his hands and prayed.

"I am here taking a stand for what I believe is right. But now I am afraid. The people are looking to me for leadership, and if I stand before them without strength and courage, they too will falter. I am at the end of my powers. I have nothing left. I've come to the point where I can't face it alone."

He describes in *Stride Toward Freedom* what happened next. His prayer was answered.

"At that moment I experienced the presence of the Divine as I had never experienced Him before. It seemed as though I could hear the quiet assurance of an inner voice saying, 'Stand up for righteousness, stand up for truth; and God will be at your side forever.' Almost at once my fears began to go. My uncertainty disappeared. I was ready to face anything."

Prayer is a marvelous and necessary supplement of our feeble efforts, but it is a dangerous substitute.

—*The Strength to Love*, p. 122

The idea that man expects God to do everything leads inevitably to a callous misuse of prayer.

—*The Strength to Love*, p. 122
(see Biography 1956, GOD)

PRESIDENT

No President can be great, or even fit for office, if he attempts to accommodate to injustice to maintain his political balance.

> —Speech, New York City, September 12, 1962
> (see KENNEDY ASSASSINATION, LEADER)

PRESSURE

I must say to you that we have not made a single gain in civil rights without determined legal and nonviolent pressure.

> —Letter from Birmingham Jail, 1963
> (see ACTIVISM, AGITATION, TENSION)

PRIORITIES

We need a radical reordering of our national priorities.

> —Chicago Freedom Movement statement, March 28, 1967

Let's face the fact. Most of us are going to be living in the ghetto five, ten years from now. But we've got to get some things straightened out right away. I'm not going to wait a month to get the roaches out of my house.

> —Article in *The Nation*, September 19, 1966, p. 240
> (see SOCIETY, WORLD REVOLUTION)

PRISON

Dr. King was arrested 125 times and spent many long days and nights behind prison walls for his beliefs. When he was sentenced to four months at Reidsville State Prison in Georgia after his arrest at an Atlanta sit-in, he said to reporters, "This is the cross that we must bear for the freedom of our people."

On Wednesday afternoon, October 26, 1960, he wrote his first letter from prison to his wife Coretta.

Hello Darling,

Today I find myself a long way from you and the children. . . . I know this whole experience is very difficult for you to adjust to, especially in your condition of pregnancy, but as I said to you yesterday this is the cross that we must bear for the freedom of our people. . . .

I have the faith to believe that this excessive suffering that is now coming to our family will in some little way serve to make Atlanta a better city, Georgia a better state, and America a better country.

Just how I do not yet know, but I have faith to believe it will. If I am correct then our suffering is not in vain.

I understand that everybody—white and colored—can have visitors this coming Sunday. I hope you can find some way to come down. . . .

Please bring the following books to me: *Stride Toward Freedom*, Paul Tillich's *Systematic Theology* Vol. 1 and 2, George Buttrick's *The Parables of Jesus*, E. S. Jones' *Mahatma Gandhi, Horns and Halo*, a Bible, a Dictionary and my reference dictionary called *Increasing Your Word Power*. . . .

Give my best regards to all the family. Please ask them not to worry about me. I will adjust to whatever comes in terms of pain. Hope to see you Sunday.

Eternally yours,
Martin

(see BIRMINGHAM JAIL, JAIL, LETTER FROM BIRMINGHAM JAIL)

PRIZE WINNER

When King was in grade school he entered a statewide public speaking contest sponsored by the Elks. It was held in Valdosta, Georgia, several hours' busride from Atlanta.

The young King traveled to the competition with his teacher and garnered second prize. Their exhilaration turned to anger, however, when they boarded the bus for the return trip to Atlanta. Although there were empty seats, none were in the Negro section. Both the student and the teacher were forced to stand up the entire trip home.

Martin Luther King never forgot this humiliating experience. He was struck by the irony that his public speaking prize meant nothing to the white people—that there would be no seat for him simply because he was black.

No one riding in that bus could have guessed that fifteen years later this young man would lead the movement that put an end to segregated seating on buses, or that twenty-five years later he would win the greatest prize that can be awarded to a living person: the Nobel Peace Prize.

(see NOBEL PRIZE)

PROGRESS

After the Birmingham victory in June of 1963, King went on a triumphant national speaking tour. He concluded a speech to a crowd of 25,000 in Los Angeles with a folksy homily to progress: "I say good night to you by quoting the words of an old Negro slave. 'We ain't what we want to be and we ain't what we're going to be. But thank God we ain't what we was.' "

Human progress is neither automatic nor inevitable. Even a superficial look at history reveals that no social advance rolls in on the wheels of inevitability. Every step toward the goal of justice requires sacrifice, suffering, and struggle; the tireless exertions and passionate concern of dedicated individuals.

—*Stride Toward Freedom*, p. 197

Human progress never rolls in on wheels of inevitability;
it comes through the tireless efforts of men willing to be
co-workers with God, and without this hard work, time itself becomes an ally of the forces of social stagnation.

—Letter from Birmingham Jail, 1963
(see ACTIVISM, GOD, HISTORY, SIN)

PROMISED LAND

We are bound for the promised land. We shall taste the
milk of freedom and the honey of equality.

—Speech at a rally, Chicago, August 5, 1966
(see BELOVED COMMUNITY, KINGDOM OF GOD)

PROTEST

He who passively accepts evil is as much involved in it as
he who helps to perpetrate it. He who accepts evil without
protesting against it is really cooperating with it.

—*Stride Toward Freedom*, p. 51

We are at the moment when our lives must be placed on
the line if our nation is to survive its own folly. Every man
of humane convictions must decide on the protest that
best suits his convictions, but we must all protest.

—*The Trumpet of Conscience*, p. 31
(see CIVIL DISOBEDIENCE, NONCOOPERATION)

PUBLIC RELATIONS

Public relations is a very necessary part of any protest of
civil disobedience. The main objective is to bring moral
pressure to bear upon an unjust system or a particularly
unjust law. The public at large must be aware of the ineq-
uities involved in such a system.

—Letter to Harold Courlander, October 30, 1961
(see EXPOSURE, MASS MEDIA)

R

RACE

The problem of race is America's greatest moral dilemma.

—*Stride Toward Freedom*, p. 205

The idea of a superior or inferior race is a myth that has been completely refuted by anthropological evidence.

—*Stride Toward Freedom*, p. 206

RACE PREJUDICE

Softmindedness is one of the basic causes of race prejudice.

—*The Strength to Love*, p. 4

Race prejudice is based on groundless fears, suspicions and misunderstandings.

—*The Strength to Love*, p. 4

All prejudice is evil, but the prejudice that rejects a man because of the color of his skin is the most despicable expression of man's inhumanity to man.

—*Where Do We Go from Here?* p. 110

Racial prejudice is a blatant denial of the unity which we have in Christ, for in Christ there is neither Jew nor Gentile, bond nor free, Negro nor white.

—*The Strength to Love*, p. 97

RACISM

Racism and its perennial ally—economic exploitation—provide the key to understanding most of the international complications of this generation.

—*Where Do We Go from Here?* p. 173

Racism is total estrangement. It separates not only bodies, but minds and spirits. Inevitably it descends to inflicting spiritual or physical homicide upon the out-group.

—*Where Do We Go from Here?* p. 70

History has shown that, like a virulent disease germ, racism can grow and destroy nations.

—*Where Do We Go from Here?* p. 93

For too long the depth of racism in American life has been underestimated. The surgery to extract it is necessarily complex and detailed. As a beginning it is important to X-ray our history and reveal the full extent of the disease.

—*Why We Can't Wait*, p. 119

The racism of today is real, but the democratic spirit that has always faced it is equally real.

—*Where Do We Go from Here?* p. 83
(see AMERICA, ECONOMIC INJUSTICE, FEAR, MATERIALISM)

RECONCILIATION

We cannot be satisfied with a court "victory" over our white brothers.... We must act in such a way as to make possible a coming together of white people and colored people on the basis of a real harmony of interests and understanding. We seek an integration based on mutual respect.... We must now move from protest to reconciliation.

—*Stride Toward Freedom*, pp. 171–72
(see BELOVED COMMUNITY, CHRISTIAN LOVE,
INTEGRATION, SYNTHESIS)

REFORM

Laws are passed in a crisis mood after a Birmingham or a Selma, but no substantial fervor survives the formal signing of legislation. The recording of the law in itself is treated as the reality of the reform.

—*Where Do We Go from Here?* p. 5
(see GOVERNMENT, LAW)

RELIGION

Any religion that professes to be concerned with the souls of men and is not concerned with the slums that damn them, the economic conditions that strangle them, and the social conditions that cripple them, is a dry-as-dust religion. Such a religion is the kind the Marxists like to see—an opiate of the people.

—*Stride Toward Freedom*, p. 36

A religion true to its nature must also be concerned about man's social conditions. Religion deals with both earth and heaven, both time and eternity. Religion operates not only on the vertical plane but also on the horizontal. It seeks not only to integrate men with God but to integrate men with men and each man with himself.

—*Stride Toward Freedom*, p. 36

It well has been said: "A religion that ends with the individual, ends."

—*Stride Toward Freedom*, p. 91
(see CHRISTIANITY, CHURCH, SCIENCE VERSUS RELIGION)

RETALIATION

During the Montgomery Bus Boycott there were many acts and threats of violence from whites directed against blacks. King urged the blacks not to succumb to the temptation of retaliation.

One night at a mass meeting in Montgomery he said to the assembly: "If one day you find me sprawled and dead, I do not want you to retaliate with a single act of violence. Remember, if I am stopped, this movement will not be stopped, because God is with this movement. I urge you to continue protesting with the same dignity and discipline you have shown so far. The old law of an eye for an eye leaves everybody blind."

To meet hate with retaliatory hate would do nothing but intensify the existence of evil in the universe.

—*Stride Toward Freedom*, p. 87

The potential beauty of human life is constantly made ugly by man's ever-recurring song of retaliation.

—*The Strength to Love*, p. 27

Along the way of life, someone must have sense enough and morality enough to cut off the chain of hate.

—*Stride Toward Freedom*, p. 104
(see EVIL, HATRED, LOVE, NONVIOLENCE)

REVENGE

In spite of the fact that the law of revenge solves no social problems, men continue to follow its disastrous leading. History is cluttered with the wreckage of nations and individuals that pursued this self-defeating path.

—*The Strength to Love*, p. 29
(see NONVIOLENCE, RETALIATION, WAR)

REVOLUTION

During the Birmingham protest in 1963, King was accused of trying to start a revolution. Rather than deny the charge that he was using "revolutionary" tactics, he freely admitted it.

"Indeed, we are engaged in a social revolution," he avowed, "and while it may be different from other revolutions, it is a revolution just the same. It is a movement to bring about certain basic structural changes in the architecture of American society. This is certainly revolutionary. My only hope is that it will remain a nonviolent revolution."

A social movement that only moves people is merely a revolt. A movement that changes both people and institutions is a revolution.

—*Why We Can't Wait*, p. 117

The summer of 1963 was a revolution because it changed the face of America. Freedom was contagious. Its fever boiled in nearly one thousand cities, and by the time it

193

had passed its peak, many thousands of lunch counters, hotels, parks and other places of public accommodation had become integrated.

—*Why We Can't Wait*, p. 117

We do not have much time. The revolutionary spirit is already world-wide. If the anger of the peoples of the world at the injustice of things is to be channeled into a revolution of love and creativity, we must begin now to work, urgently, with all the peoples, to shape a new world.

—*The Trumpet of Conscience*, p. 50

Our only hope today lies in our ability to recapture the revolutionary spirit and go out into a sometimes hostile world declaring eternal opposition to poverty, racism and militarism.

—*Where Do We Go from Here?* p. 190
(see AMERICAN REVOLUTION, NEW WORLD ORDER, WORLD REVOLUTION)

RIGHT

"I can't promise you that it won't get you beaten! I can't promise you that it won't get your house bombed!" bellowed Martin Luther King to a crowd at Brown Chapel before the Selma march began. "I can't promise you won't get scarred up a bit! But we must stand up for what is right!"

There is nothing to be afraid of if you believe and know that the cause for which you stand is right. You are ready to face anything and you face it with a humble smile on your face, because you know that all of eternity stands with you and the angels stand beside you and you know you are right.

—Speech, Savannah, Georgia, January 1, 1961
(see PRAYER, SELMA, WRONG)

RIOTS

When the Black Power movement was rising and King was losing popularity among his people, he stood before a group of civil rights workers in Chicago in 1966 and said: "Even if every Negro in the United States comes to think that Negroes ought to riot, I'm going to stand as that lone voice and say, 'It's impractical, it's unsound, and we'll never get our own way that way.' "

A riot is at bottom the language of the unheard. It is the desperate, suicidal cry of one who is so fed up with the powerlessness of his cave existence that he asserts that he would rather be dead than ignored.

—*Where Do We Go from Here?* p. 112

At best the riots have produced a little anti-poverty money being allotted by frightened government officials, and a few water-sprinklers to cool the children of the ghettos. It is something like improving the food in a prison while the people remain securely incarcerated behind bars. Nowhere have the riots won any concrete improvement such as have the organized protest demonstrations.

—*Where Do We Go from Here?* pp. 57–58

The ultimate weakness of a riot is that it can be halted by superior force. We have neither the techniques, the numbers, nor the weapons to win a violent campaign.

—Quoted in "King Tells Goals," Chicago *Tribune*, July 11, 1966

Social justice and progress are the absolute guarantors of riot prevention. There is no other answer.

—*Where Do We Go from Here?* p. 22

(see BLACK POWER, DEMONSTRATION, REVOLUTION, VIOLENCE)

SALVATION

Neither God nor man will individually bring the world's salvation. Rather, both Man and God, made one in a marvelous unity of purpose through an overflowing of love . . . can transform the old into the new and drive out the deadly cancer of sin.

—The Strength to Love, p. 124
(see EVIL, GOD, SIN)

SCIENCE

When scientific power outruns moral power, we end up with guided missiles and misguided men. When we foolishly minimize the internal of our lives and maximize the external, we sign the warrant for our own day of doom.

—Where Do We Go from Here? p. 172

We have come to see that science can give us only physical power, which, if not controlled by spiritual power, will lead inevitably to cosmic doom.

—*The Strength to Love,* p. 56
(see ALIENATION, GODS, SCIENCE VERSUS RELIGION, TECHNOLOGY)

SCIENCE VERSUS RELIGION

Science investigates: religion interprets. Science gives man knowledge which is power; religion gives man wisdom which is control. Science deals mainly with facts; religion deals mainly with values. The two are not rivals. They are complementary. Science keeps religion from sinking into the valley of crippling irrationalism and paralyzing obscurantism. Religion prevents science from falling into the marsh of obsolete materialism and moral nihilism.

—*The Strength to Love,* p. 3
(see also GODS, MATERIALISM, RELIGION)

SEGREGATION

Any law that degrades human personality is unjust. All segregation laws are unjust because segregation distorts the soul and damages the personality. It gives the segregator a false sense of superiority and the segregated a false sense of inferiority.

—Letter from Birmingham Jail, 1963

Segregation scars the soul of both the segregator and the segregated. The segregator looks upon the segregated as a thing to be used, not a person to be respected. Segregation substitutes an "I-it" relationship for the 'I-thou" relationship. Thus it is utterly opposed to the noble teachings of the Judeo-Christian tradition.

—*Stride Toward Freedom,* p. 205

Two segregated souls never meet in God. Segregation denies the sacredness of human personality.

—*Where Do We Go from Here?* p. 97

Segregation is also morally wrong because it deprives man of freedom, the quality which makes him man.

—*Where Do We Go from Here?* p. 97

Segregation is dead. The only question remaining is how costly the funeral will be.

—*The Strength to Love*, p. 104

Segregation will end in my lifetime.

—Speech at Gandhi Society dinner, May 17, 1962
(see DESEGREGATION, INTEGRATION, SYNTHESIS)

SELF-CRITICISM

One of the sure signs of maturity is the ability to rise to the point of self-criticism.

—*Stride Toward Freedom*, p. 223
(see CRITICISM)

SELF-ESTEEM

As long as the mind is enslaved the body can never be free. Psychological freedom, a firm sense of self-esteem, is the most powerful weapon against the long night of physical slavery.

—*Where Do We Go from Here?* p. 43

The Negro must boldly throw off the manacles of self-abnegation and say to himself and the world: "I am somebody. I am a person. I am a man with dignity and honor.

I have a rich and noble history, however painful and exploited that history has been. I am black *and* comely."

—*Where Do We Go from Here?* pp. 43–44
(see BEAUTY, INFERIORITY COMPLEX)

SELF-HELP

The Negro must come to see that there is much he himself can do about his plight. He may be uneducated or poverty-stricken, but these handicaps must not prevent him from seeing that he has within his being the power to alter his fate.

—*Stride Toward Freedom*, p. 211
(see ACTIVISM, ECONOMIC REFORM, EDUCATION)

SELF-RIGHTEOUSNESS

You must come to see that a man may be self-centered in his self-denial and self-righteous in his self-sacrifice. His generosity may feed his ego and his piety, his pride. Without love, benevolence becomes egotism and martyrdom becomes spiritual pride.

—*The Strength to Love*, pp. 133–34

SELF-SACRIFICE

During the first weeks of the Montgomery bus boycott, Dr. King received daily death threats from white racists. On Monday night, January 14, 1956, during a church meeting King surprised the assembly with an emotional outburst. In the middle of a prayer he shouted out, "Lord, I hope no one will have to die as a result of our struggle for freedom in Montgomery. But if anyone has to die, let it be me!"

After this exclamation he was helped to his chair by several associates. King received much criticism over the years for his morbid references to his own willingness to sacrifice his life for the cause. But his words proved prophetic, while his willingness to make the ultimate self-sacrifice was undoubtedly an inspiration to others to follow his courageous example.

(see COURAGE)

SELMA

When he arrived in Selma on March 6, 1965, the night before the scheduled march, King was told of the court injunction against the march. "We've gone too far to turn back now," he said at a rally that night. "We must let them know that nothing can stop us—not even death itself. We must be ready for a season of suffering."

Close associates of King have said that he expected to be killed during the Selma March. He had received many death threats, and he knew he would be an easy target at the front of the long line of marchers.

When he arrived at the departure point, Brown Chapel, at 2:25 p.m. the next afternoon, he greeted a crowd of three thousand. "We have the right to walk the highways," he told the crowd. "I have no alternative but to lead a march from this spot to carry our grievances to the seat of government. I have made my choice. I have got to march. I do not know what lies ahead of us. There may be beatings, jailings, tear gas. But I would rather die on the highways of Alabama than make a butchery of my conscience."

He paused, then added: "I ask you to join me today as we move on." They joined him, five abreast down Sylvan Street.

But this march was halted in a confrontation with Alabama State troopers at Pettus Bridge. It was a tense confrontation. King made a difficult decision not to risk a violent confrontation. After a prayer ceremony, he turned the march around and returned to the church. He vowed to try again.

That night a white minister, Reverend James Reeb, a participant in the march, was severely beaten by a group of white racists. The minister died at 6:55 a.m. the next morning. The three men who were later indicted for the murder were all acquitted by a Selma jury.

Confrontations, discussions, and negotiations continued throughout the week of Reeb's death. The following Monday, March 15, President Johnson made a speech to Congress urging passage of the voting rights bill. He spoke of Selma: "What happened in Selma is part of a far larger movement which reaches into every section and state of America. It is the effort of the American Negroes to secure for themselves the full blessings of American life."

That day Judge Johnson persuaded Sheriff Jim Clark to allow an integrated march along a prescribed route in Selma. The march was scheduled to begin March 21.

"Walk together, children, don't you get weary, and it will lead us to the Promised Land," King exhorted the three thousand marchers at the outset. "And Alabama will be a new Alabama, and America will be a new America."

Five days later the march reached Montgomery, its final destination, where twenty-five thousand more marchers joined them. At the conclusion of the march, Martin Luther King stood proudly and defiantly on the steps of the Alabama State capitol and delivered a fiery oration:

"They told us we wouldn't get here. And there were those who said that we would get here only over their dead bodies, but all the world knows that we are here and that we are standing before the forces of power in the state of Alabama, saying, 'We ain't goin' let nobody turn us around.'

"Last Sunday more than eight thousand of us started on a mighty walk from Selma, Alabama. We have walked on meandering highways and rested our bodies on rocky byways.

"I can say as Sister Pollard said ... who lived in this community during the bus boycott. One day she was asked while walking if she didn't want a ride, and when she answered 'No,' the person said, 'Well, aren't you tired?' and with ungrammatical profundity, she said, 'My feets is tired, but my soul is rested.' "

King spoke of the purpose of the Selma March as a demonstration of the necessity for voting registration reform.

"Our whole campaign in Alabama has been centered around the right to vote.... The threat of the free exercise of the ballot by the Negro and white masses alike resulted in the establishing of a segregated society. They segregated Southern money from the poor whites; they segregated Southern churches from Christianity; they segregated Southern minds from honest thinking, and they segregated the Negro from everything."

King tried to assure his people that they were on the move now and that they would not be stopped.

"My people, my people, listen! The battle is in our hands.

"I know some of you are asking today, 'How long will it take?' I come to say to you this afternoon however difficult the moment, however frustrating the hour, it will not be long, because truth pressed to earth will rise again.

"How long? Not long, because no lie can live forever.

"How long? Not long, because you will reap what you sow.

"How long? Not long, because the arm of the moral universe is long but it bends toward justice."

(see Biography 1965, INJUNCTION, MARCHING RHETORIC)

SERMON

The sermon was the medium for Martin Luther King's message. He developed the sermon to the level of an art form. He was one of history's greatest performers of the sermon. The pulpit was the platform from which King delivered most of his speeches, but even when he was not speaking in church his orations were usually modified sermons.

In his senior year at Morehouse College, after deciding to pursue a career as a preacher, King began to develop the sermonizing style that would carry him to fame and, ultimately, immortality. College classmates recalled that "Tweedie," as King was nicknamed because of his penchant for tweed suits, had already acquired some of his characteristic showmanship—for example, his habit of closing his sermon folder just before stepping to the pulpit, so that everyone could see he was preaching without his notes. His father, the Reverend Martin Luther King, Sr., objected to this affectation, believing that a pastor should preach from a manuscript. The younger King, however, preferred to speak extemporaneously at least some of the time. In his greatest orations, including his triumphant address at the March on Washington, he spoke with the confidence of one who has come to the podium with a written text committed to memory, but is also willing to speak extemporaneously when and if the spirit moves him.

Coretta Scott King recollected that in his first year as a minister Dr. King would spend fifteen hours a week preparing the Sunday sermon, first writing it out completely, then memorizing it. However, as he became busier and he settled into a schedule of speaking several times a week, there was not enough time to prepare each sermon or speech ahead of time. In later years he would usually prepare an outline of his three or four main topics and sermonize from the outline.

There has been some controversy in recent years about King's alleged use of unattributed quotations in his early papers and sermons. Perhaps Ralph Abernathy is correct when he says King "stole" some of his ideas and metaphors from older works:

"I use the word 'stole' here in the same way T.S. Eliot used it when he said that the mark of a mature poet is when he stops borrowing from other poets and starts stealing outright. Martin would study the homilies of earlier clergymen, take what he could use out of them, and then turn them into new and contemporary sermons, speaking them in his own idiom with his own voice."

As King matured, he developed his own original voice, relying less upon his spiritual predecessors.

(see Biography 1963, DREAM, PRIZE WINNER)

SERVICE

At the heart of Martin Luther King's philosophy was the idea of *service*. Service is the soul's highest purpose. Service is the path to happiness, to greatness, and to God. And *anyone* can serve.

"You don't have to have a college degree to serve," according to King. "You don't have to make your subject and your verb agree to serve. You don't have to know about Plato and Aristotle to serve. You don't have to know Einstein's theory of relativity to serve. You don't have to know the second theory of thermodynamics in physics to serve. You only need a heart full of grace. A soul generated by love."

(see GREATNESS, SUCCESS)

SHOES

Dr. King and Reverend Abernathy were sitting on the stage at an Ivy League university, listening patiently while the president was introducing Ralph, who was supposed to introduce Martin to the jammed auditorium.

The president was going on and on, as college presidents are sometimes inclined to do, and Martin, who was able to find humorous relief in even the stuffiest situations, elbowed Ralph.

"Look at that man's shoes," he whispered.

Ralph looked at the university president's shoes and noticed that when the speaker rose up on his toes to make a lofty point, he revealed that both his shoes had holes in the soles.

In a low voice Martin quoted "Amazing Grace." "It looks as if those shoes are saying, 'Through many dangers, toils and snares I have already come.'"

Just at that moment, the college president completed his introduction and turned to Abernathy. All eyes were on Abernathy, who rose, red-faced with laughter, and strode self-consciously to the podium, while King looked on with a straight face, dignified as always.

(see AGE, HUMOR, ICE CREAM, SNORE)

SIN

King preached that man alone could not overcome sin; nor could man leave it to God alone to remove sin; that only man working *together* with God could overcome sin.

"Many of you here know something of what it is to struggle with sin," he said in a sermon on March 3, 1963. "Year by year you became aware of the terrible sin that was taking possession of your life. It may have been slavery to drink, untruthfulness, the impurity of selfishness or sexual promiscuity. And as the years unfolded the vice grew bolder and bolder.

"You said to yourself, 'One day I'm going to rise up and drive this evil out. I know it is wrong. It is destroying my character and embarrassing my family.'

"At last the day came and you made a New Year's resolution that would get rid of the whole base evil. And then the next year came around and you were doing the same old evil thing.

"And out of amazement you found yourself asking, 'Why could I not cast it out?' And in this moment of despair you decided to take your problem to God....

"Even after taking the problem to God, however, the evil did not go away. 'You discovered that the evil was still with you. God would not cast it out.' "

"If neither man nor God could remove evil alone, what was the solution? A partnership between man and God. Human beings must allow God to work through them.

"God would not cast it out, for he never removes sin without the cordial cooperation of the sinner."

One cannot remove an evil habit by mere resolution nor by simply calling on God to do the job, but only as he surrenders himself and becomes an instrument of God.

—*The Strength to Love*, p. 125

Evil is not driven out, but crowded out . . . through the expulsive power of something good.

—"How a Christian Overcomes Evil," exam paper, January 9, 1953

SINNER

"When I delve into the inner chambers of my own being," King confessed to his congregation in a sermon on December 10, 1967, "I end up saying, 'Lord, be merciful unto me, a sinner.' "

We are all sinners on earth, according to King. It is the duality of human existence. "There are times that all of us know somehow that there is a Mr. Hyde and a Dr. Jekyll in us."

But God will not judge us for our separate sins. "God does not judge us by the separate incidents or the separate mistakes we make, but by the total bent of our lives.

"You don't need to go out this morning saying Martin Luther King is a saint," said the preacher who had only four months left to live. "I want you to know this morning that I am a sinner like all of God's children, but I want to be a good man, and I want to hear a voice saying to me one day, 'I take you in and I bless you because you tried.' "

(see DUALISM, EVIL, HIGHER SELF, SIN)

SNEEZE

The night before his assassination, April 3, 1968, Dr. King delivered his last speech to a crowd of two thousand at the Masonic temple in Memphis. In that speech King recalled being stabbed in a Harlem bookstore ten years earlier, and how the blade had come so close to his heart that his surgeon had told him if he had sneezed, it would have killed him.

While he was recuperating in the hospital he received a get-well letter from a white schoolgirl in New York state who said: "I read in the paper that the doctor said if you had even sneezed, you would have lost your life. I am glad you did not sneeze and that God spared you to continue to do good."

"And I want to say tonight that I too am happy that I didn't sneeze. Because if I had sneezed, I wouldn't have been around here in 1960, when students from all over the South started sitting-in at lunch counters. And I knew as they were sitting in, they were really standing up for the best in the American dream, and taking the whole nation back to those great wells of democracy which were dug deep by the founding fathers in the Declaration of Independence and the Constitution.

"If I had sneezed, I wouldn't have been around in 1961, when we decided to take a ride for freedom, and ended segregation in interstate travel.

"If I had sneezed, I wouldn't have been around in 1962, when Negroes in Albany, Georgia, decided to straighten their backs up. And whenever men and women straighten their backs up, they are going somewhere, because a man can't ride your back unless it is bent.

"If I had sneezed, I wouldn't have been around here in 1963, when the black people of Birmingham, Alabama, aroused the conscience of the nation and brought into being the civil rights bill.

"If I had sneezed, I wouldn't have had the chance later that year, in August, to try to tell America about a dream that I had had.

"If I had sneezed, I wouldn't have been down in Selma, Alabama, to see the great movement there.

"If I had sneezed, I wouldn't have been in Memphis to see a great community rally around those brothers and sisters who are suffering.

"I'm so glad I didn't sneeze."

(see Biography 1968, ASSASSINATION)

SNORE

King was a lover of liberty and loathed jail. However, imprisonment was an inevitable consequence of the civil disobedience he preached. One way he coped with the stress

of repeated arrests was by using humor. Companions recall that King would tease Abernathy about his snoring.
During the Birmingham campaign, King was nervous
about the prospect of getting arrested.

"If I have to get arrested," he said, eyeing Abernathy,
"let me get arrested with people who don't snore."

Abernathy vehemently denied the charge. "I do *not*
snore!"

"You are *torture!*" King replied, with a twinkle in his
eye. "White folks ain't *invented* anything that can get to me
like you do. *Anything* they want me to admit to, I will, if
they'll just get you and your snoring out of my cell."

(see BIRMINGHAM, HUMOR, JAIL, PRISON)

SOCIAL CHANGE

Above all, our experience has shown that social change
can take place without violence.

—Stride Toward Freedom, p. 188
(see NOBEL PRIZE, REVOLUTION)

SOCIETY

We must rapidly begin the shift from a "thing"-oriented
society to a "person"-oriented society. When machines and
computers, profit motives and property rights are considered more important than people, the giant triplets of racism, materialism and militarism are incapable of being
conquered.

—Where Do We Go from Here? p. 186
(see MATERIALISM, PRIORITIES, TECHNOLOGY)

SOUL

Our generation cannot escape the question of our Lord:
What shall it profit a man, if he gain the whole world of

externals—airplanes, electric lights, automobiles, and color television—and lose the internal—his own soul?

—*The Strength to Love,* p. 57
(see ALIENATION, MATERIALISM, PERSONALITY)

STUDENTS

King gave students a lot of credit for the successes of the civil rights movement. When students began organizing sit-ins to protest segregation in the South in 1960, it launched an era of student activism. King praised the students:

"What is fresh, what is new in your fight is the fact that it was initiated, led, and sustained by students. What is new is that American students have come of age. You now take your honored places in the world-wide struggle for freedom."

(see EDUCATION, YOUTH)

STUPIDITY

We have a mandate both to conquer sin and also to conquer ignorance. Modern man is presently having a rendezvous with chaos, not merely because of human badness, but also because of human stupidity.

—*The Strength to Love,* p. 32
(see CHAOS, EDUCATION, RACE PREJUDICE)

SUCCESS

We are prone to judge success by the index of our salaries or the size of our automobiles, rather than by the quality of our service and relationship to humanity.

—*Stride Toward Freedom,* p. 94
(see GREATNESS, SERVICE)

SUFFERING

"Unearned suffering is redemptive." This was one of the fundamental principles of Martin Luther King's creed. Suffering experienced by nonviolent resisters of injustice was unearned and therefore redemptive, both individually and collectively.

We must somehow believe that unearned suffering is redemptive.

—Speech on front porch in Montgomery, after bombing of the King home, January 30, 1956 (see CHRISTIANITY, NONVIOLENCE)

SUPERFICIALITY

The Darwinian concept of the survival of the fittest has been substituted by a philosophy of the survival of the slickest.

—*The Strength to Love*, p. 44

SYNTHESIS

Synthesis was the key to Martin Luther King's philosophy. King used synthesis to resolve difficult philosophical, ideological, and sociopolitical issues. Synthesis was derived from the dialectical method made famous by the German philosopher Hegel, known for his formulation "thesis-antithesis-synthesis."

King tried to avoid the extremes, which he saw as the thesis and the antithesis. He sought the synthesis that combined the two. He avoided extreme "either-or" viewpoints about black and white, rich and poor, communism and capitalism, materialism and humanism, pessimism and optimism, liberalism and conservatism, and so forth. Instead of "either-or" he sought the "both-and" solution of synthesis by combining conflicting contraries to create a greater, more harmonious whole, a synthesis.

Integration was one form of synthesis championed by King as a solution to racial conflict; nonviolent resistance was another form of synthesis King championed as a solution to social injustice.

Like the synthesis in Hegelian philosophy, the principle of nonviolent resistance seeks to reconcile the truths of two opposites—acquiescence and violence—while avoiding the extremes and immoralities of both.

—*Stride Toward Freedom*, p. 213

The truth about man is found neither in the thesis of pessimistic materialism nor the antithesis of optimistic humanism, but in a higher synthesis. Man is neither villain nor hero; he is rather both villain and hero.

—*The Strength to Love*, p. 88

The Kingdom of God is neither the thesis of individual enterprise nor the antithesis of collective enterprise, but a synthesis which reconciles the truth of both.

—*The Strength to Love*, p. 99

An adequate understanding of man is found neither in the thesis of liberalism nor in the antithesis of neoorthodoxy, but in a synthesis which reconciles the truths of both.

—*The Strength to Love*, p. 136

Like the synthesis of Hegelian philosophy, the realistic attitude seeks to reconcile the truths of two opposites and avoid the extremes of both.

—"A Realistic Look at the Question of Progress in the Area of Race Relations," in Boston Collection, quoted in Smith and Zepp

Jesus recognized the need for blending opposites. . . . And he gave them a formula for action: "Be ye therefore wise as serpents and harmless as doves" . . . To have serpentlike qualities devoid of dovelike qualities is to be passionless, mean, and selfish. To have dovelike without serpentlike qualities is to be sentimental, anemic and aimless. We must combine the strongly marked antithesis.

—*The Strength to Love*, pp. 1, 5

Life at its best is a creative synthesis of opposites in fruitful harmony.

—*The Strength to Love*, p. 1
(see DIALECTICAL METHOD)

TACTICS

Tactics are to be used only so long as they are effective in achieving specific goals. They should be subjected to frequent analysis, review and evaluation. Tactics should be modified in response to the ever changing situations that confront us.

—President's annual report to SCLC convention, October 1, 1964

TAXES

In 1959 Martin Luther King was charged by the state of Alabama with filing fraudulent tax returns for 1956 and 1958. He denied the charges, but privately expressed fears that this official attempt to discredit him might succeed in reducing his credibility as a moral leader.

"Many people will think I am guilty," he said sadly. "And so, for the rest of my life, people will believe that I took money that didn't belong to me."

Coretta had never seen him so troubled. "I tried desperately to assure him that the vast majority of the people believed in him and understood the motivation of the state of Alabama."

The case came to trial in May 1959. The state charged that King had perjured himself in claiming a 1956 income of $9,150 and a 1958 income of $25,248. At issue were charges that he derived large personal sums from his civil rights activities, for which he did not pay taxes.

King contended that, although he had protested the figures, he had paid the disputed amount to the state in 1958. In the course of the trial the check he had written to Alabama for the disputed amount was discovered. The check had never been cashed. On May 28, 1959, the all-white jury returned a verdict of not guilty.

TECHNOLOGICAL PROGRESS

When the less sensitive supporters of the status quo try to argue against some of these condemnations and challenges, they usually cite the technological marvels our society has achieved. However, that only reveals their poverty of spirit. . . . Nothing in our glittering technology can raise man to new heights, because material growth has been made an end in itself, and, in the absence of moral purpose, man himself becomes smaller as the works of man become bigger.

—*The Trumpet of Conscience*, p. 43
(see ALIENATION, INTERNAL VERSUS EXTERNAL, SCIENCE)

TEENAGER

King liked to tell the story of the teenage boy who decided to join the demonstrations in Birmingham. The teenager's father did not want him to get arrested and forbade him to go.

"I don't want to disobey you, Daddy, but I have made

my pledge," said the teenager. "If you try to keep me home, I will sneak off. If you think I deserve to be punished for that, I'll just have to take the punishment. You see, I'm not doing this only because I want to be free. I'm doing it also because I want freedom for you and Mama, and I want it to come before you die."

The father reflected on this and gave his son his blessing.

(see WALKING)

TENSION

Innate in all life and all growth is tension. Only in death is there an absence of tension. To cure injustices, you must expose them before the light of human conscience and the bar of public opinion, regardless of whatever tensions that exposure generates.

—Playboy Interviews, 1967, p. 356

I am not afraid of the word "tension." I have earnestly opposed violent tension, but there is a type of constructive, nonviolent tension which is necessary for growth.

—Letter from Birmingham Jail, 1963

We who engage in nonviolent direct action are not the creators of tension. We merely bring to the surface the hidden tension that is already alive. We bring it out in the open where it can be seen and dealt with.

—Letter from Birmingham Jail, 1963
(see CRISIS, EXPOSURE, INJUSTICE, PRESSURE)

THIRD WORLD

During his trip to India in 1957, King was appalled by the poverty he saw; it was worse than anything he'd seen in the United States. "How can one avoid being depressed when one sees with one's own eyes evidence of millions of people going to bed hungry at night?" he asked in his Christmas eve sermon of 1967. "How can one avoid being depressed when one sees with one's own eyes thousands of people sleeping on sidewalks at night? More than a million people sleep on the sidewalks of Bombay every night; more than half a million sleep on the sidewalks of Calcutta every night. They have no houses to go into. They have no beds to sleep in. As I beheld these conditions, something within me cried out: 'Can we in America stand idly by and not be concerned?' And an answer came: 'Oh, no!' And I started thinking about the fact that right here in our country we spend millions of dollars every day to store surplus food; and I said to myself: 'I know where we can store that food free of charge—in the wrinkled stomachs of the millions of God's children in Asia, Africa, Latin America, and even in our nation, who go to bed hungry at night.' "

King was sympathetic to the newly independent nations of Africa and the Third World. He asked the citizens of the developed nations to be tolerant and understanding of the growing pains of the undeveloped nations. He urged that the West recognize its moral obligation to provide economic assistance.

We must use our vast resources of wealth to aid the undeveloped countries of the world. Have we spent far too much of our national budget in establishing military bases around the world and far too little in establishing bases of genuine concern and understanding?

—*The Strength to Love*, p. 73

We in the West must bear in mind that the poor countries are poor primarily because we have exploited them through political or economic colonialism.

—*The Trumpet of Conscience*, p. 62

Ultimately a great nation is a compassionate nation.

—*Where Do We Go from Here?* p. 178
(see WESTERN NATIONS, WORLD REVOLUTION)

THREAT

King and the other leaders of the civil rights movement lived under the constant threat of violence. In fact, King had to live not with the possibility of violence but the *certainty* of violence.

During the first month of the Montgomery Bus Boycott, King's house was bombed. A few days later King and Reverend Ralph Abernathy were discussing the situation.

"The one thing that worries me is the possibility that they might bomb my church," admitted Abernathy. "It's an historic building, and I would hate to think that anything I did would lead to its destruction."

King, his voice charged with emotion, replied: "Ralph, make no mistake about it. Your church *will* be bombed. It will be bombed."

This prediction came true a few weeks later when Abernathy's church was one of four churches in Montgomery bombed by white racists in one night. The churches were damaged, but fortunately no one was injured in the blasts.

"You were right," said Abernathy, informing King of the news. King sighed. "I was hoping I was wrong."

(see BOMBING)

TIME

We must get rid of the false notion that there is some miraculous quality in the flow of time that inevitably heals all evils.

—Where Do We Go from Here? p. 128
(see PROGRESS)

TOKENISM

The tokenism Negroes condemn is recognizable because it is an end in itself. Its purpose is not to begin a process, but instead to end the process of protest and pressure.

—Why We Can't Wait, pp. 31–32

Tokenism is a promise to pay. Democracy, in its finest sense, is payment.

—Why We Can't Wait, p. 31
(see DEMOCRACY, NOW)

TRAVEL

King was a tireless traveler. In an average year his travel, according to an estimate published by *Crusader* magazine, totaled approximately 780,000 miles. If this figure is accurate, he spent enough time in airplanes and cars to circle the globe thirty times a year. Even if that figure was grossly exaggerated, it is well-documented that King attended approximately two hundred speaking engagements a year. In other words, he gave a public speech of some sort, somewhere or other, just about every other night of his adult life. His extensive speaking schedule kept him away from home more than half the time.

TRIAL SERMON

Martin Luther King was in his junior year of college when he decided to become a preacher like his father. His parents were under the impression that he was planning to be a lawyer, so they were surprised by his announcement.

"Are you serious about this?" asked Daddy King.

"Yessir, I'm going to preach," said Martin, who was then eighteen.

"You won't make any money preaching," warned his father.

"I'll preach for nothing," replied the young man. "I'm not going to worry about money."

Daddy King decided it was necessary to test his son's resolve. "I'll arrange a trial sermon for you here."

The aspiring young preacher was taken aback. His father's Ebenezer Baptist Church was the largest congregation in the South. "Can't I try my wings in a smaller church first?"

"Let's find out if you have any wings."

So it was agreed that Martin Luther King, Jr., would preach a trial sermon at Ebenezer Baptist Church.

On the night of the trial sermon the church was filled. The sermon was a rousing success, recalled Daddy King. "But I didn't congratulate him afterward. I went off into the sanctuary and I got down on my knees and I thanked the Lord for giving me such a son."

(see Biography 1953–55, SERMON)

TRUTH

He who lives with untruth lives in spiritual slavery. Freedom is still the bonus we receive for knowing the truth.

—*Where Do We Go from Here?* p. 67

I believe that unarmed truth and unconditional love will have the final word in reality.

—Nobel address, December 11, 1964
(see EVIL, GOD, HISTORY)

U

UNDERPRIVILEGED

I choose to identify with the underprivileged. I choose to identify with the poor. I choose to give my life for the hungry. I choose to give my life for those who have been left out of the sunlight of opportunity.... This is the way I'm going. If it means suffering a little bit, I'm going that way. If it means sacrificing, I'm going that way. If it means dying for them, I'm going that way, because I heard a voice saying, "Do something for others."

—Sermon, "The Good Samaritan," August 28, 1966
(see SERVICE)

UNEMPLOYMENT

The United States teetered on the edge of revolution in the 1930s when unemployment ranged up to 25 percent. Today in the midst of historic prosperity unemployment for Negro youth, according to government figures, runs as high as 30 to 40 percent in many cities. With most of their lives yet to live, the slamming of doors in their faces can be expected to induce rage and rebellion.

—*The Trumpet of Conscience*, p. 11.

Let us do one simple, direct thing—let us end unemployment totally and immediately. I propose specifically the creation of a national agency that shall provide a job to every person who needs work.

—Telegram to President Johnson, July 25, 1967
(see ECONOMIC INJUSTICE,
GUARANTEED NATIONAL INCOME, POVERTY)

UNITED NATIONS

The United Nations is a gesture in the direction of nonviolence on a world scale.

—*Where Do We Go from Here?* p. 184
(see NOBEL PRIZE, WORLD PERSPECTIVE)

UNITED STATES

The mere fact that we live in the United States means that we are caught in a network of inescapable mutuality. Therefore no American can afford to be apathetic about the problem of racial justice.

—*Stride Toward Freedom*, p. 199

Anyone who lives inside the United States can never be considered an outsider anywhere within its bounds.

—Letter from Birmingham Jail, 1963
(see AMERICA, INTERDEPENDENCE)

UNITY

There is amazing power in unity. Where there is true unity, every effort to disunite only serves to strengthen the unity.

—Stride Toward Freedom, p. 150

The plea for unity is not a call for uniformity. There must always be healthy debate.

Where Do We Go from Here? p. 124
(see DIVISION, SYNTHESIS)

UNIVERSE

I am convinced that the universe is under the control of a loving purpose, and that in the struggle for righteousness man has cosmic companionship.

—The Strength to Love, p. 94

The universe is on the side of justice.

—Stride Toward Freedom, p. 106
(see GOD, MORALITY)

VICTIMS

We must not let the fact that we are the victims of injustice lull us into abrogating responsibility for our own lives.

Stride Toward Freedom, p. 223
(see SELF-HELP)

VICTORY

A final victory is an accumulation of many short-term encounters. To lightly dismiss a success because it does not usher in a complete order of justice is to fail to comprehend the process of achieving full victory. It underestimates the value of confrontation and dissolves the confidence born of a partial victory by which new efforts are powered.

—*Where Do We Go from Here?* pp. 12–13
(see PROGRESS)

"The promises of the Great Society have been shot down on the battlefield of Vietnam," said King to a Los Angeles audience in February 1967. The government had shifted its attention and its resources from the War on Poverty at home to the war in Vietnam.

"We spend $322,000 for each enemy we kill, while we spend in the so-called war on poverty in America only about $53 for each person we classify as 'poor.' "

In addition to all the physical casualties of the Vietnam War, the ideals and hopes of a generation were dying in the war in Southeast Asia, said King, and the nation's commitment and enthusiasm for civil rights was dying, too. The Nobel Peace laureate concluded his address by urging his listeners to merge the civil rights movement with the peace movement: "We must combine the fervor of the civil rights movement with the peace movement."

King had been warned by other civil rights leaders that he would hurt the movement if he publicly announced his opposition to the Vietnam War. But his conscience would not allow him to remain silent any longer. He could not continue to be a champion of nonviolence at home without declaring his opposition to violence abroad.

On April 4, 1967, exactly a year before his death, he delivered a forceful sermon at Manhattan's Riverside Church, which marked a turning point in the national dialogue on the war.

"As I have walked among the desperate, rejected, angry young men, I have told them that Molotov cocktails and rifles would not solve their problems. I have tried to offer them my deepest compassion, while maintaining my conviction that social change comes most meaningfully through nonviolent action. But, they asked, and rightly so, what about Vietnam? They asked if our own nation wasn't using massive doses of violence to solve its problems, to bring about the changes it wanted. Their questions hit home, and I knew that I could never again raise my voice against the violence of the oppressed in the ghettos without having first spoken clearly to the greatest purveyor of violence in the world today: my own government." The American involvement in Vietnam was nothing less than "madness," he said. "Somehow, this madness must cease."

King was so widely criticized for his stand on Vietnam that he lost much of the popular support and prestige that was the foundation of his leadership. The establishment press, which had been sympathetic to him until then, now seemed to turn against him. A *New York Times* reviewer wrote that King's antiwar speech "has dampened his prospects for becoming the Negro leader who might be able to get the nation 'moving again' on civil rights." A Washington *Post* editorial pronounced, "Many who have listened to him with respect will never again accord him the same confidence." *Life* magazine referred to his Riverside sermon as "demagogic slander."

However, there was one man who was converted by that sermon—King's own father. Many fathers and sons disagreed about Vietnam. Martin Luther King, Sr., had tried for months to dissuade his son from speaking out against the war, saying it would be a terrible mistake for the civil rights movement. "When he finished his great speech, I knew," said King's father, "the whole audience knew—the man was right."

Today, young men of America are fighting, dying, and killing in Asian jungles in a war whose purposes are so ambiguous the whole nation seethes with dissent. They are told they are sacrificing for democracy, but the Saigon regime, their ally, is a mockery of democracy, and the black American soldier has himself never experienced democracy.

—*The Trumpet of Conscience*, p. 37

This business of burning human beings with napalm, of filling our nation's homes with orphans and widows, of injecting poisonous drugs of hate into the veins of peoples normally humane, of sending men home from dark and bloody battlefields physically handicapped and psychologically deranged, cannot be reconciled with wisdom, justice, and love.

—*The Trumpet of Conscience*, pp. 32–33

The war in Vietnam is but a symptom of a far deeper malady within the American spirit.

—*The Trumpet of Conscience*, p. 32
(see JOHNSON, PEACE, WAR)

VIOLENCE

Violence as a way of achieving racial justice is both impractical and immoral.

It is impractical because it is a descending spiral ending in destruction for all. The old law of an eye for an eye leaves everybody blind.

It is immoral because it seeks to humiliate the opponent rather than to win his understanding; it seeks to annihilate rather than to convert.

Violence is immoral because it thrives on hatred rather than love. It destroys community and makes brotherhood impossible. It leaves society in monologue rather than dialogue.

Violence ends by defeating itself. It creates bitterness in the survivors and brutality in the destroyers.

—*Stride Toward Freedom*, p. 213

If the American Negro and other victims of oppression succumb to the temptation of using violence in the struggle for freedom, future generations will be the recipients

of a desolate night of bitterness, and our chief legacy to
them will be an endless reign of meaningless chaos. Violence is not the way.

—*Stride Toward Freedom*, p. 213

Violence is the antithesis of creativity and wholeness. It
destroys community and makes brotherhood impossible.

—*Where Do We Go from Here?* p. 61
(see HATRED, RETALIATION)

VIOLENT REBELLION

The courageous efforts of our own insurrectionist brothers,
such as Denmark Vesey and Nat Turner, should be eternal
reminders to us that violent rebellion is doomed from the
start.... Beyond the pragmatic invalidity of violence is its
inability to appeal to conscience. Power and morality must
go together, implementing, fulfilling, and ennobling each
other.

—*Where Do We Go from Here?* pp. 68–69
(see BLACK POWER, MALCOLM X, RIOTS)

VOTE

"We can never be satisfied as long as a Negro in Mississippi cannot vote," King contended in 1964, "and a Negro
in New York believes he has nothing for which to vote."

The chief weapon in our fight for civil rights is the vote. I
can foresee the Negro vote becoming the decisive vote in
national elections.

—At meeting of Montgomery Improvement Association
during Montgomery Bus Boycott, May 1956
(see APATHY, JOHNSON, SELMA)

WAITING

For years now we have heard the word "Wait!" It rings in the ear of every Negro with piercing familiarity. This "Wait" has almost always meant "Never." We must come to see, with one of our most distinguished jurists, that "justice too long delayed is justice denied."

Perhaps it is easy for those who have never felt the stinging darts of segregation to say, "Wait." But when you have seen vicious mobs lynch your mothers and fathers at will and drown your sisters and brothers at whim; when you have seen hate-filled policemen curse, kick, and even kill your black brothers and sisters; when you see the vast majority of your twenty million Negro brothers smothering in an airtight cage of poverty in the midst of an affluent society . . . when you are forever fighting a degenerating sense of "nobodiness"—then you will understand why we find it difficult to wait.

—Letter from Birmingham Jail, 1963
(see SELF-ESTEEM)

WALKING

King liked to tell the story of an elderly lady who refused a ride during the Montgomery Bus Boycott. A car-pool driver pulled up alongside the old lady and said, "Jump in, grandmother. You don't need to walk." She waved him on. "I'm not walking for myself," she told the driver. "I'm walking for my children and my grandchildren." She kept on walking.

(see MONTGOMERY, SELMA, TEENAGER)

WAR

Wisdom born of experience should tell us that war is obsolete. There may have been a time when war served as a negative good by preventing the spread and growth of an evil force, but the destructive power of modern weapons eliminates even the possibility that war may serve as a negative good.

—The Strength to Love, p. 29

I knew that America would never invest the necessary funds or energies in rehabilitation of its poor so long as adventures like Vietnam continued to draw men and skills and money like some demoniacal destructive suction tube. And so I was increasingly compelled to see the war not only as a moral outrage but also as an enemy of the poor, and to attack it as such.

—The Trumpet of Conscience, pp. 22–23
(see PEACE, VIETNAM, WAR)

WEDDING

Before their wedding ceremony—held at the Scotts' house in Marion, Alabama—Martin and Coretta Scott were taken aside for a private talk by Martin Luther King, Sr., who had at first opposed the match in his desire to see his son wedded to the daughter of a more prominent Atlanta family.

"It's not too late to call this thing off," said Daddy King, "and I advise you to call it off now ... unless—"

"Unless what?" asked Martin, glancing at an anxious Coretta.

"Unless you simply can't help it," said Daddy King. "I preach because I can't help myself. When you get married you should think of it that way, as something you are impelled to do. Think about this for a few minutes and decide if this is the way you feel. I don't want to go through with this ceremony unless you feel you can't help yourselves."

Daddy King left the astonished bride and bridegroom alone in the room and closed the door. Coretta looked at Martin querulously. He grinned. "That's the little talk he always gives young couples before he marries them."

Martin and Coretta went ahead with the wedding. At Coretta's request, the promise of the wife to obey her husband was removed from the wedding vows—she argued that it was inequitable—and Daddy King, who performed the ceremony, grudgingly obliged her.

After the reception, the newlyweds departed on their honeymoon by car. Coretta did the driving while Martin, exhausted, slumped over in the passenger seat and slept.

(see CORETTA, FIRST DATE, HONEYMOON)

WESTERN NATIONS

It is a sad fact that because of comfort, complacency, a morbid fear of communism, and our proneness to adjust to injustice, the Western nations that initiated so much of the revolutionary spirit of the modern world have now become the arch-antirevolutionaries. This has driven many to feel that only Marxism has the revolutionary spirit. Therefore, communism is a judgment against our failure to make democracy real and follow through on the revolutions that we initiated.

—*The Trumpet of Conscience*, p. 33
(see COMMUNISM, DEMOCRACY, WORLD REVOLUTION)

WHITE

Negroes hold only one key to the double lock of peaceful change. The other is in the hands of the white community.

—*Where Do We Go from Here?* p. 22

In the final analysis the white man cannot ignore the Negro's problem, because he is a part of the Negro and the Negro is a part of him. The Negro's agony diminishes the white man, and the Negro's salvation enlarges the white man.

—*Where Do We Go from Here?* p. 101

Both Negro and white workers are equally oppressed. For both, the living standards need to be raised to levels consistent with our national resources.

—*Stride Toward Freedom*, pp. 203–4

WORLD PERSPECTIVE

We must develop a world perspective. No individual can live alone; no nation can live alone, and as long as we try, the more we are going to have war in this world.

—*The Trumpet of Conscience*, p. 68
(see INTERDEPENDENCE, LOYALTY, MANKIND)

WORLD REVOLUTION

A worldwide revolution is in progress, according to King. "Look at just about any place in the world and the exploited people are rising against their exploiters," he told the press during the Montgomery Bus Boycott in 1955. "This seems to be the outstanding characteristic of our generation."

King warned that the United States, the initiator of the democratic revolution that began in the west in 1776 and is spreading throughout the world today, is ironically in danger of aligning itself on the wrong side of the world revolution now and thereby forfeiting its legacy of greatness.

I am convinced that if we are not to get on the right side of the world revolution, we as a nation must undergo a radical revolution of values.

A true revolution of values will soon cause us to question the fairness and justice of many of our past and present policies.

A true revolution of values will soon look uneasily on the glaring contrast between poverty and wealth. With righteous indignation, it will look across the seas and see individual capitalists of the West investing huge sums of money in Asia, Africa, and South America only to take the profits out with no concern for the social betterment of the countries, and say: "This is not just."

It will look at our alliance with the landed gentry of Latin America and say: "This is not just."

The Western arrogance of feeling that it has everything to teach others and nothing to learn from them is not just.

A true revolution of values will lay hands on the world

order and say of war: "This way of settling differences is not just."

—*The Trumpet of Conscience*, p. 32
(see NOBEL PRIZE, THIRD WORLD, WESTERN NATIONS)

WRONG

On the first day of the Montgomery Bus Boycott, Dr. King assured the black people of Montgomery that as Americans they had the right to protest injustice.

"The only weapon that we have in our hands this evening is the weapon of protest," he told the crowd at the Holt Street Baptist Church on the night of December 5, 1955. "If we were incarcerated behind the curtain of a communistic nation—we couldn't do this. If we were trapped in the dungeon of a totalitarian regime—we couldn't do this. But the great glory of American democracy is the right to protest for right."

The crowd roared its approval. He continued:

"We are not wrong in what we are doing. If we are wrong—the Supreme Court of this nation is wrong. If we are wrong—God Almighty is wrong!

"If we are wrong—Jesus of Nazareth was merely a utopian dreamer and never came down to earth!

"If we are wrong—justice is a lie!"

(see RIGHT)

X

X, MALCOLM

King, as an integrationist, was critical of the separatism preached by Black Muslims. In August of 1960, Malcolm X wrote a letter to King inviting him to hear Black Muslim leader Elijah Muhammad at a Harlem rally. The letter was sent to the wrong address and arrived late.

Through his secretary, King politely declined the late invitation with a letter that began wryly: "Dear Mr. X".

(see MALCOLM X)

Y

YOUNG PEOPLE

During the darkest days of the Montgomery Bus Boycott, Martin Luther King, who was himself a young man in his twenties, called out to the generations of young people who would come in the future. King wanted future generations of young people to know that it was the youth of his own time who made the great change. "I want young men and young women who are not alive today but who will come into this world with new privileges and new opportunities—I want them to know and see that these new privileges and opportunities did not come without somebody suffering and sacrificing for them."

It is difficult to exaggerate the creative contribution of young Negroes. They took nonviolent resistance, first employed in Montgomery, Alabama, in mass dimensions, and developed original forms of applications—sit-ins, freedom rides, and wade-ins. To accomplish these, they first transformed themselves.

—*The Trumpet of Conscience*, p. 46

Young Negroes had traditionally imitated whites in dress, conduct, and thought in a rigid, middle-class pattern. . . . Now they ceased imitating and began initiating. Leadership passed into the hands of Negroes, and their white allies began learning from them. This was a revolutionary and wholesome development for both.

—*The Trumpet of Conscience*, p. 46

The blanket of fear was lifted by Negro youth. When they took their struggle to the streets, a new spirit of resistance was born. Inspired by the boldness of and ingenuity of Negroes, white youth stirred into action and formed an alliance that aroused the conscience of the nation.

—*The Trumpet of Conscience*, p. 45

A BRIEF BIOGRAPHY
OF MARTIN LUTHER KING, JR.

~ 1929 ~

He is born Michael Luther King in Atlanta on January 15, 1929, the middle child of three, in his parents' bedroom in the home of his maternal grandfather, Reverend A. D. Williams. His father is then known as Mike King and his mother is Alberta Williams King.

~ 1934 ~

Michael King, Sr., officially changes his own name to Martin Luther King and his son's name to Martin Luther King, Jr.

"M.L.," as the boy is called, first becomes aware of racism when a white playmate is told by a parent not to play with him.

He told me one day that his father had demanded that he would play with me no more. I will never forget what a great shock this was to me. I immediately asked my parents about the motive behind such a statement. We were at the dinner table when the situation was discussed, and here, for the first time, I was made aware of the existence of a race problem. I had never been conscious of it before.

Every parent at some time faces the problem of explaining the facts of life to his child. Just as inevitably, for the Negro parent, the moment comes when he must explain to his offspring the facts of segregation. My mother took me on her lap and began by telling me about slavery and how it had ended with the Civil War. She tried to explain the divided system of the South—the segregated schools, restaurants, theaters, housing; the white and colored signs on drinking fountains, waiting rooms, lavatories—as a social condition rather than a natural order. Then she said the words that almost every Negro hears before he can yet understand the injustice that makes them necessary: "You are as good as anyone."

My mother, as the daughter of a successful minister, had grown up in comparative comfort. She had been sent to the best available school and college and had, in general, been protected from the worst blights of discrimination. But my father, a sharecropper's son, had met its brutalities at first hand, and had begun to strike back at an early age.

~ 1935–40 ~

Two childhood incidents impressed M.L. with his father's moral courage in stranding up against racism.

I remember a trip to a downtown store with my father when I was still small. We sat down in the first empty seats at the front of the store. A young white clerk came up and murmured politely:

"I'll be happy to wait on you if you'll just move to those seats in the rear."

My father answered, "There's nothing wrong with these seats. We're quite comfortable here."

"Sorry," said the clerk, "but you'll have to move."

"We'll either buy shoes sitting here," my father retorted, "or we won't buy shoes at all." Whereupon he took me by the hand and walked out of the store. This was the first time I'd ever seen my father so angry. I still remember walking down the street beside him as he muttered, "I don't care how long I have to live with this system, I will never accept it."

And he never has. I remember riding with him another day when he accidentally drove past a stop sign. A policeman pulled up to the car and said:

"All right, boy, pull over and let me see your license."

My father replied indignantly, "I'm no boy." Then, pointing to me, "This is a boy. I'm a *man*, and until you call me one, I will not listen to you."

The policeman was so shocked that he wrote the ticket up nervously, and left the scene as quickly as possible.

~ 1943–46 ~

During my early teens I was deeply concerned by the problems of racial justice.... The first time that I was seated behind a curtain in a dining car I felt as though the curtain had been dropped on my selfhood. I also learned that the inseparable twin of racial injustice is economic injustice. I saw how the systems of segregation exploited both the Negro and poor whites. These early experiences made me deeply conscious of the varieties of injustice in our society.

During my late teens I worked two summers, against my father's wishes—he never wanted my brother and me to work around white people because of the oppressive conditions—in a plant that hired both Negroes and whites. Here I saw economic injustice firsthand, and realized that the poor white was exploited just as much as the Negro.

* * *

Seeking early admission to Morehouse College, MLK completes a battery of tests, and is admitted, skipping his senior year of high school.

He enters magnolia-shaded Morehouse College at the age of fifteen, attending classes during the day while continuing to live at home with his parents.

His first introduction to the literature on nonviolence and civil disobedience comes in a philosophy class at Morehouse.

> When I went to Atlanta's Morehouse College as a freshman in 1944 my concern for racial and economic justice was already substantial. During my student days at Morehouse I read Thoreau's *Essay on Civil Disobedience* for the first time. Fascinated by the idea of refusing to cooperate with an evil system, I was so deeply moved that I reread the work several times. This was my first intellectual contact with the theory of nonviolent resistance.

Although MLK only reads at an eighth-grade level when he enters college, he improves rapidly and becomes a prominent student within two years.

He rises to prominence as an orator, winning the Webb Oratorical Contest in his sophomore year.

~ 1947 ~

During his junior year, at the age of 17, MLK announces his decision to follow in his father's footsteps and become a minister.

> I had felt the urge to enter the ministry from my latter high school days, but accumulated doubts had somewhat

blocked the urge. Now it appeared again with an inescapable drive. My call to the ministry was not a miraculous or supernatural something; on the contrary, it was an inner urge calling me to serve humanity. I guess the influence of my father also had a great deal to do with my going in the ministry. This is not to say that he ever spoke to me in terms of being a minister, but that my admiration for him was the great moving factor. He set forth a noble example that I didn't mind following.

~ 1948 ~

MLK publishes his first article, a piece titled "The Purpose of Education," in the Morehouse College campus newspaper.

> The function of education, therefore, is to teach one to think intensively and to think critically. But education which stops with efficiency may prove the greatest menace to society. The most dangerous criminal may be the man gifted with reason, but with no morals.
>
> —"The Purpose of Education," *Maroon Tiger*, 1948

Prior to graduation, MLK is chosen by President Mays and the faculty of Morehouse to speak for his class in the annual student oratory event.

> There are moral laws of the universe that man can no more violate with impunity than he can violate its physical laws.
>
> —Morehouse annual student oration, 1948

In the spring of 1948 MLK applies to Crozer Theological Seminary in Chester, Pennsylvania, a primarily white Baptist seminary known for its liberal-leaning theology. He is accepted.

After graduating from Morehouse College in June 1948, he moves north to Pennsylvania.

I gained my major influences from ... Morehouse and Crozer—and I feel greatly indebted to them. They gave me the basic truths I now believe ... the idea of the oneness of humanity and the dignity and worth of all human personality.... At Crozer I found the actual living out of Christian beliefs.

Not until I entered Crozer Theological Seminary in 1948, however, did I begin a serious intellectual quest for a method to eliminate social evil. Although my major interest was in the fields of theology and philosophy, I spent a great deal of time reading the works of the great social philosophers.

At Crozer MLK works hard to prove himself as a student and to avoid being stereotyped as a Negro.

I was well aware of the typical white stereotype of the Negro, that he is always late, that he's loud and always laughing, that he's dirty and messy, and for a while I was terribly conscious of trying to avoid identification with it.... Rather than be thought of as always laughing, I'm afraid I was grimly serious for a time. I had a tendency to overdress, to keep my room spotless, my shoes perfectly shined and my clothes immaculately pressed.

MLK takes every course he can on the subject of oratory and sermonizing: a total of nine courses at Crozer.

In the fall of 1948 he visits Fellowship House at the University of Pennsylvania and is inspired by a guest lecture on Gandhi.

One Sunday afternoon I traveled to Philadelphia to hear a sermon by Dr. Mordecai Johnson, president of Howard

245

University. . . . Dr. Johnson had just returned from a trip to India, and, to my great interest, he spoke of the life and teachings of Mahatma Gandhi. His message was so profound and electrifying that I left the meeting and went out and bought a half-dozen books on Gandhi's life and works.

Gandhi's philosophy provides for King the missing link between Christianity and social reform.

It was in this Gandhian emphasis on love and nonviolence that I discovered the method for social reform that I had been seeking for so many months. . . . I came to feel that this was the only morally and practically sound method open to oppressed people in their struggle for freedom.

~ 1951–53 ~

Graduating from Crozer in June of 1951, MLK wins the Pearl Plafker Award as the most outstanding student and is awarded the J. L. Lewis Crozer fellowship for graduate study.

Turned down by Yale, MLK is accepted by Boston University, where he enrolls for doctoral study.

At Boston University he studies religion with Edgar Brightman and Harold DeWolf, leaders of the philosophy of Personalism, which will have a lasting influence on his thought.

I studied philosophy and theology at Boston University under Edgar S. Brightman and L. Harold DeWolf. Both men greatly stimulated my thinking. It was mainly under these teachers that I studied personalistic philosophy—the theory that the clue to the meaning of ultimate reality is found in personality. This personal idealism remains today my basic philosophical position. Personalism's insistence that only personality—finite and infinite—is ultimately real strengthened me in two convictions: it gave me metaphysical and philosophical grounding for the idea of a personal God, and it gave me a metaphysical basis for the dignity and worth of all human personality.

MLK meets Coretta Scott, a music student from Alabama, and proposes to her on the first date. Coretta is hesitant at first but after repeated proposals she accepts.

Martin and Coretta are married in the garden of Coretta's parents' home in Marion, Alabama, on June 18, 1953.

August of 1953, after being in school twenty-one years without a break, I had reached the satisfying moment of completing the residential requirements for the Ph.D. degree. The major job that remained was to write my doctoral thesis. In the meantime I had felt that it would be wise to start considering a job so that I could be placed at least by September 1954. . . .

I had received a letter from the officers of the Dexter Avenue Baptist Church of Montgomery, saying that they were without a pastor and that they would be glad to have me preach when I was again in that part of the country.

~ 1954 ~

In January 1954, MLK preaches a trial sermon at the Dexter Avenue Baptist Church in Montgomery, Alabama.

I was very conscious this time that I was on trial. How should I best impress the congregation? . . . Should I attempt to interest it with a display of scholarship? Or should I preach just as I had always done, depending finally on the inspiration of the spirit of God? I decided to follow the latter course. I said to myself, "Keep Martin Luther King in the background and God in the foreground and everything will be all right. Remember you are a channel of the Gospel and not the source."

The sermon, titled "The Three Dimensions of a Complete Life," is a success, and MLK is offered the appointment as pastor.

The question of my wife's musical career came up. She was certain that a Northern city would afford a greater opportunity for continued study than any city in the deep South. For several days we talked and thought and prayed over each of these matters. Finally we agreed that, in spite of the disadvantages and inevitable sacrifices, our greatest service could be rendered in our native South.

In Montgomery, MLK follows an energetic regimen, arising at 5:30 a.m. to work for three hours on his dissertation, then putting in a full day's work at the church.

~ 1955 ~

MLK completes his Ph.D. dissertation, "A Comparison of the Conceptions of God in the Thinking of Paul Tillich and Henry Nelson Wieman" and becomes Dr. Martin Luther King.

First child Yolanda Denis (Yoki) is born November 17.

After the arrest of Rosa Parks on December 1, King joins the movement to boycott the segregated buses.

As I thought further I came to see that what we were really doing was withdrawing our cooperation from an evil system, rather than merely withdrawing our economic

248

support from the bus company. . . . At this point I began to think about Thoreau's *Essay on Civil Disobedience*. I remembered how, as a college student, I had been moved when I first read this work. I became convinced that what we were preparing to do in Montgomery was related to what Thoreau had expressed. We were simply saying to the white community, "We can no longer lend our cooperation to an evil system."

On December 5, King is surprised to find himself elected President of the newly formed Montgomery Improvement Association, which makes him the official spokesman for the boycott.

As soon as Rev. Roy Bennet had opened the nominations for President, Rufus Lewis spoke from the corner of the room: "Mr. Chairman, I would like to nominate Reverend M. L. King for president." The motion was seconded and carried, and in a matter of minutes I was unanimously elected.

The action had caught me unawares. It had happened so quickly that I did not even have time to think it through. It is probable that if I had, I would have declined the nomination.

MLK rushes home to tell his wife and to prepare for a mass rally at seven o'clock, where he will be expected to speak.

She did not need to be told that we would now have even less time together, and she seemed undisturbed at the possible danger to all of us in my new position. "You know," she said quietly, "that whatever you do, you have my backing."

Reassured, I went to my study and closed the door. The minutes were passing fast . . . I had only twenty minutes to prepare the most decisive speech of my life. As I thought of the limited time before me and the possible implications of the speech, I became possessed by fear. . . . I turned to God in prayer. . . .

What could I say to keep them courageous and prepared for positive action and yet devoid of hate and resentment? . . .

I decided that I had to face the challenge head on, and attempt to combine two irreconcilables. I would seek to arouse the group to action by insisting that their self-respect was at stake and that if they accepted such injustices without protesting, they would betray their own sense of dignity and the eternal edicts of God Himself. But I would balance this with a strong affirmation of the Christian doctrine of love.

MLK arrives at Holt Street Church to find five thousand people outside. Inside the church is so packed he must be passed above the crowd to reach the pulpit. He delivers an electrifying speech.

We are here this evening for serious business. On so many occasions Negroes have been intimidated and humiliated and oppressed because of the sheer fact that they were Negroes.

Just the other day, just last Thursday to be exact, one of the finest citizens in Montgomery—not one of the finest Negro citizens, but one of the finest citizens in Montgomery—was taken from a bus and carried to jail and arrested because she refused to get up and give her seat to a white person.

We are going to work together right here in Montgomery. When the history books are written in the future, somebody will have to say, "There lived a race of people, of black people, of people who had the moral courage to stand up for their rights. And thereby they injected new meaning into the veins of history, and of civilization." And we're gonna do that. God grant that we will do it before it's too late.

MLK's speech evokes a powerful response, reverberating through Montgomery and across the nation, ultimately touching the nerve of a generation.

> As I sat listening to the continued applause I realized that this speech had evoked more response than any speech or sermon I had ever delivered, and yet it was virtually unprepared. I came to see for the first time what the older preachers meant when they said, "Open your mouth and God will speak for you."

Soon there is backlash from the white community. King receives many death threats.

> And then we started our struggle together. Things were going well for the first few days, but then, ten or fifteen days later, after the white people in Montgomery knew that we meant business, they started doing some nasty things. They started making nasty telephone calls, and it came to the point that some days more than forty telephone calls would come in, threatening my life, the life of my family, the life of my child.

~ 1956 ~

On January 26, MLK is arrested for speeding, the first in a series of harrassing police actions against him.

He is released on bail, but the next morning, after being awakened by a death threat, he reaches a low point of despair. He prays and his prayer is answered dramatically (see PRAYER). It is his first transcendental religious experience.

> And it seemed at that moment that I could hear an inner voice saying to me, "Martin Luther, stand up for righ-

teousness. Stand up for justice. Stand up for truth. And lo
I will be with you, even to the end of the world" ...
I heard the voice of Jesus saying still to fight on. He
promised never to leave me, never to leave me alone. No
never alone. No never alone. He promised never to leave
me, never to leave me alone.

Despite innumerable death threats and the bombing of his
house, MLK maintains his nonviolent leadership of the
boycott.

On November 13 a decision by the Supreme Court declares bus segregation illegal, ensuring victory for the boycott.

Now a seasoned leader at the age of 27, MLK announces
the end of the boycott and declares that the past year had
taught them six lessons.

[1] We have discovered that we can stick together for a
common cause; [2] Our leaders do not have to sell out;
[3] Threats and violence do not necessarily intimidate
those who are sufficiently aroused and nonviolent; [4] Our
church is becoming militant, stressing a social gospel as
well as a gospel of personal salvation; [5] We have gained
a new sense of dignity and destiny; [6] We have discovered a new and powerful weapon—nonviolent resistance.

~ 1957 ~

King calls a meeting of sixty black ministers in New Or-
leans on February 14. A new organization is formed to
fight segregation and achieve civil rights: the Southern
Christian Leadership Conference. MLK is unanimously
elected president.

MLK makes his first national address on May 17, in a civil rights rally in the nation's capital. In front of a crowd of 15,000, he calls for voting rights reform.

Second child Martin Luther III (Marty) is born on October 23.

~ 1958 ~

On June 23, King meets President Eisenhower.

He is arrested on September 3 in front of the courthouse and charged with loitering. Convicted, MLK says he will go to jail rather than pay the fine. The fine is paid by Police Commissioner Clyde Sellers.

King's first book, *Stride Toward Freedom*, is published on September 17, 1958, to excellent reviews. He goes on a national publicity tour to promote it.

During the tour MLK is nearly killed when he is stabbed in a store in Harlem on September 20.

I sat in a Harlem department store, surrounded by hundreds of people. I was autographing copies of *Stride Toward Freedom*, my book about the Montgomery bus boycott of 1955–56. As I signed my name to a page, I felt something sharp plunge forcefully into my chest. I had been stabbed with a letter opener, struck home by a woman who would later be judged insane. Rushed by ambulance to Harlem Hospital, I lay in a bed for hours while preparations were made to remove the keen-edged knife from my body. Days later, when I was well enough to talk with Dr. Aubrey Maynard, the chief of the surgeons who had performed the delicate, dangerous operation, I learned the reason for the long delay that preceded surgery. He told me that the razor tip of the instrument had been touching my aorta and that my whole chest had to be opened to extract it.

"If you had sneezed during all those hours of waiting," Dr. Maynard said, "your aorta would have been punctured and you would have drowned in your own blood."

~ 1959 ~

After recovering from the stabbing, King leaves Montgomery on February 2 with Coretta and colleague Lawrence Reddick, traveling to New Delhi for a thirty-day tour of cities and villages across India. They meet Prime Minister Nehru and study techniques of nonviolence.

I left India more convinced than ever before that nonviolent resistance is the most potent weapon available to oppressed people in their struggle for freedom. It was a marvelous thing to see the results of a nonviolent campaign.

Returning to Montgomery, King decides to retire from his pastorship in order to concentrate on civil rights full-time.

On November 29 he gives his farewell sermon to his congregation at Dexter Avenue Baptist Church.

For almost four years now I have been trying to do as one man what five or six people ought to be doing. . . . What I have been doing is giving, giving, giving and not stopping to retreat and meditate like I should—to come back. If the situation is not changed, I will be a physical and psychological wreck. I have to reorganize my personality and reorient my life. . . .

I have a sort of nagging conscience that someone will interpret my leaving Montgomery as a retreat from the civil rights struggle. Actually, I will be involved in it on a larger scale. I can't stop now. History has thrust something upon me which I cannot turn away. I should free you now.

~ 1960 ~

King is arrested, along with thirty-six others (mostly students) for insisting on being served at the lunch counter of Rich's department store in Atlanta.

On October 25 he is sentenced to serve four months of a twelve-month probationary sentence of hard labor at Reidsville State Prison.

After the intervention of John Kennedy and Robert Kennedy, he is released on October 27.

MLK expresses gratitude to the Kennedys upon his release but does not make a formal endorsement of JFK.

~ 1961 ~

King urges the newly elected Kennedy administration to make history in the civil rights arena.

The new administration has the opportunity to be the first in one hundred years of American history to adopt a radically new approach to the question of civil rights. . . . The day is past for tolerating vicious and inhuman opposition on a subject which determines the lives of 22,000,000 Americans.

Third child Dexter Scott is born on January 30.

The Freedom Riders arrive in Montgomery on May 20. When King holds a rally at the First Baptist Church, a mob of white racists surround the church. MLK and his followers are escorted to safety by federal marshals ordered there by Robert Kennedy.

In November, as a result of the Freedom Rides and King's persistent pressure, the Interstate Commerce Commission bans segregation in interstate travel.

On December 16 King is arrested in Albany, Georgia, where he is campaigning against segregation of public facilities.

~ 1962 ~

During the unsuccessful Albany movement, King is arrested again on July 27 and jailed.

On October 16 King meets with President Kennedy at the White House.

~ 1963 ~

Fourth child Bernice Albertine is born March 28.

On April 3, King and his associates launch Project C, the Birmingham campaign, which will prove to be the turning point in the war to end segregation in the South.

On Good Friday, April 12, King is arrested with Ralph Abernathy by Police Commissioner Eugene "Bull" Connor for demonstrating without a permit.

As we neared the downtown area, Bull Connor ordered his men to arrest us. Ralph and I were hauled off by two muscular policemen, clutching the backs of our shirts in handfuls. All the others were promptly arrested.

In jail Ralph and I were separated from everyone else, and later from each other.

For more than twenty-four hours I was held incommunicado, in solitary confinement. No one was permitted to visit me, not even my lawyers. Those were the longest, most frustrating and bewildering hours I have ever lived.

You will never know the meaning of utter darkness until you have lain in such a dungeon, knowing that sunlight is streaming overhead and still seeing only darkness below. You might have thought I was in the grip of a fantasy brought on by worry. I did worry. But there was more to the blackness than a phenomenon conjured by a worried mind. Whatever the cause, the fact remained that I could not see the light.

King finally is allowed to call his wife after President Kennedy intervenes with a phone call to the Birmingham officials.

Apparently the President and his brother placed calls to officials in Birmingham; for immediately after Coretta heard from them, my jailers asked me if I wanted to call her. After the president's intervention, conditions changed considerably.

King remains in jail for eleven days, drawing national attention to Birmingham. While imprisoned he writes the classic "Letter from Birmingham Jail," answering criticism from white clergymen and explaining the need for nonviolent civil disobedience.

I am in Birmingham because injustice is here. Just as the prophets of the eighth century B.C. left their villages and carried their "thus saith the Lord" far beyond the boundaries of their home towns, and just as the Apostle Paul left his village of Tarsus and carried the gospel of Jesus Christ

257

to the far corners of the Greco-Roman world, so am I compelled to carry the gospel of freedom beyond my own home town.

On May 10 the Birmingham agreement is announced. It is an acceptance of the original demands of the movement. The stores, restaurants and schools are to be desegregated, hiring of blacks implemented, charges dropped. King issues a joint statement with Ralph Abernathy and Fred Shuttlesworth:

> The acceptance of responsibility by local white and Negro leadership offers an example of a free people uniting to meet and solve their problems. Birmingham may well offer twentieth-century America an example of progressive racial relations; and for all mankind a dawn of a new day, a promise for all men; a day of opportunity and a new sense of freedom for all America.

After the Birmingham victory, King embarks on a triumphant speaking tour from New York to California, drawing large crowds.

On June 23 MLK leads 125,000 people on a Freedom Walk in Detroit.

In July a poll of civil rights leaders in *Newsweek* reveals that 95 percent regard Martin King as the most successful spokesman for the black race.

The March on Washington held August 28 is the largest civil rights demonstration in history.

> In its entire glittering history, Washington had never seen a spectacle of the size and grandeur that assembled there on August 28, 1963. Among the nearly 250,000 people who journeyed that day to the capital, there were many digni-

taries and many celebrities, but the stirring emotion came from the mass of ordinary people who stood in majestic dignity as witnesses to their single-minded determination to achieve democracy in their time. . . .

The March was the first organized Negro operation which was accorded respect and coverage commensurate with its importance. The millions who viewed it on television were seeing an event historic not only because of the subject, but because it was being brought into their homes.

The last speaker of a long afternoon, King starts out reading the speech he had stayed up all night before writing, but inspired by the crowd's response, he abandons his text at the conclusion and speaks of his dream.

I started out reading the speech. . . . Just all of a sudden— the audience response was wonderful that day—and all of a sudden this thing came to me that I have used—I'd used it many times before, that thing about "I have a dream"— and I just felt that I wanted to use it here. I don't know why, I hadn't thought about it before the speech. (SEE DREAM)

"I have a dream" is the highlight of the March. King's inspiring vision saw beyond the racial conflict, hatred, and violence to a future in which America became a promised land of freedom and equality.

After the speech King and other black leaders meet with President Kennedy.

President Kennedy is assassinated on November 22.

King meets President Johnson on December 3 for a fifty-minute conference.

~ 1964 ~

On January 3 King appears on the cover of *Time* magazine as its Man of the Year.

King is jailed for demonstrating in St. Augustine in May.

King attends the signing ceremony of the Civil Rights Act of 1964 at the White House on July 2.

During the summer King experiences his first hurtful rejection by black people when he is stoned by Muslims in Harlem.

King is awarded the Nobel Peace Prize on December 10 in Oslo, Norway. He is the youngest person ever to win the prize. (see NOBEL PRIZE).

~ 1965 ~

On February 2 King is arrested in Selma, Alabama, during a voters' rights demonstration.

On February 9 King meets with President Johnson to discuss voting rights.

On March 21 King and three thousand protesters start a five-day march from Selma to the state capital in Montgomery.

On March 26, at the completion of the Selma march, King stands on the steps of the Alabama State Capitol and addresses 25,000 marchers. (see SELMA)

After President Johnson signs the Voting Rights Act on August 6, King turns his attention to socioeconomic issues.

~ 1966 ~

On January 22, King moves into a Lawndale slum tenement at 1550 South Hamlin Avenue in Chicago, attracting national media attention to slum living conditions.

MLK announces that his three main objectives in Chicago are (1) to educate people about slum conditions (2) to organize slum-dwellers into a union to force landlords to meet their obligations and (3) to mobilize slum tenants into an army of nonviolent demonstrators.

When James Meredith is shot on June 6, the first day of a 200-mile March Against Fear through the South, King and other civil rights leaders decide to continue the march.

During the march King caucuses in Yazoo, Mississippi, with leaders of the more militant Black Power faction of the freedom movement. While in Yazoo, he is booed by some of the Black Power advocates.

> I went home that night with an ugly feeling. Selfishly I thought of my sufferings and sacrifices over the last twelve years. Why would they boo one so close to them? But as I lay awake thinking, I finally came to myself, and I could not for the life of me have less than patience and understanding for those young people. For twelve years, I and others like me had held out radiant promises of progress. I had preached to them about my dream.... Their hopes had soared. They were now booing because they felt we were unable to deliver on our promises.

* * *

On July 10, Freedom Sunday, King initiates a campaign to make Chicago an "open city," demanding an end to discrimination in housing, employment, and schools.

Chicago city officials meet with civil rights leaders for the Summit Agreement on August 26, 1966.

King's remaining victories will be only partial victories. He is grappling with ever-larger problems with ever-decreasing support. After the Chicago summer he concludes that there is a need for a different type of revolution.

> For years I labored with the idea of reforming the existing institutions of the society, a little change here, a little change there. Now I feel quite differently. I think you've got to have a reconstruction of the entire society, a revolution of values.

~ 1967 ~

King's popularity is falling. In January a Gallup Poll reveals he is no longer in the category of the Ten Most Admired Persons.

MLK's decline in popularity accelerates when on April 4, at Riverside Church in New York, he speaks out strongly in public against the war in Vietnam. (see VIETNAM)

The publication of his last book, *Where Do We Go from Here: Chaos or Community?*, is greeted with many harsh reviews. "He has been outstripped by his times," pronounces Andrew Koplind, in *The New York Review of Books*.

On July 26 King issues a joint statement with A. Philip Randolph and Whitney Young calling for an end to the riots that "have proved ineffective and damaging to the civil rights cause and the entire nation."

In the first major judicial reversal since 1954, the Supreme Court upholds a conviction of Martin Luther King by a Birmingham court for demonstrating without a permit. In October, King spends four days in Birmingham jail along with a number of other civil rights leaders.

On November 27 King announces the inception of the Poor People's Campaign, focusing on jobs and freedom for the poor of all races.

In a Christmas eve sermon, King looks back on the years following the declaration of his dream in 1963. He expresses his disappointment at the tragedies and reversals since the March on Washington. But he concludes by reaffirming his dream.

> In 1963, on a sweltering August afternoon, we stood in Washington, D.C., and talked to the nation about many things. Toward the end of that afternoon, I tried to talk to the nation about a dream that I had had, and I must confess to you today that not long after talking about that dream I started seeing it turn into a nightmare.
>
> I saw that dream turn into a nightmare as I watched my black brothers and sisters in the midst of anger and understandable outrage, in the midst of their hurt, in the midst of their disappointment, turn to misguided riots to try to solve that problem. I saw that dream turn into a nightmare as I watched the war in Vietnam escalating. . . .
>
> Yes, I am personally the victim of deferred dreams, of blasted hopes, but in spite of that I close today by saying I still have a dream. . . .

~ 1968 ~

King announces plans for the Poor People's Campaign to culminate in the Poor People's March on Washington in April. The key demands will be a $12 billion Economic Bill of Rights guaranteeing employment to all the able-bodied, incomes to those unable to work, and an end to housing discrimination.

> We will place the problems of the poor at the seat of the government of the wealthiest nation in the history of mankind. If that power refuses to acknowledge its debt to the poor, it will have failed to live up to its promise to insure "life, liberty, and the pursuit of happiness" to its citizens.

When black sanitation workers go on strike in Memphis on February 12, King offers his support.

On March 28 King leads a march of eight thousand people in Memphis—an event that turns violent. It is a stunning blow to the nonviolent movement, for no march in which King participated had ever turned violent before.

King resolves to schedule another nonviolent march, more carefully planned, for early April to show that "nonviolence is not dead." He meets with the leaders of the Invaders, a militant gang that had participated in the March 28 riot. He receives promises of their cooperation in a nonviolent march.

On April 3, the eve of his death, King speaks at the Masonic temple in Memphis. His impromptu speech concludes with unforgettable words.

> I left Atlanta this morning, and as we got started on the plane—there were six of us—the pilot said over the public address system, "We're sorry for the delay, but we have

264

Dr. Martin Luther King on the plane, and to be sure that nothing would be wrong with the plane, we had to check out everything carefully. And we've guarded the plane all night. . . ."

Men, for years now, have been talking about war and peace. But now no longer can they just talk about it. It is no longer a choice between violence and nonviolence in this world, it's nonviolence or nonexistence.

. . . I don't know what will happen now. We've got some difficult days ahead. But it really doesn't matter with me now, because I've been to the mountaintop. And I don't mind. Like anybody, I would like to live a long life; longevity has its place. But I'm not concerned about that now. I just want to do God's will. And He's allowed me to go up to the mountain. And I've looked over. And I've seen the promised land.

I may not get there with you. But I want you to know tonight that we as a people will get to the promised land. And I'm happy tonight. I'm not worried about anything. I'm not fearing any man. Mine eyes have seen the glory of the coming of the Lord.

At sunset on April 4 Martin Luther King is fatally shot while standing on the balcony of his motel room in Memphis.

There are riots and disturbances in 130 American cities. Sixty-five thousand national guard troops are called out to quell the disturbances. There are twenty thousand arrests.

King's funeral on April 9 is an international event (see FUNERAL).

Within a week of the assassination, the Open Housing Act (called the Civil Rights Act of 1968) is passed by Congress at the urging of President Johnson, who wrote in his memoirs, "That legislation might have ultimately passed anyway, but it is entirely possible that Martin Luther King bought it with his life."

Two weeks after the assassination, the city of Memphis yields to the demands of the striking black sanitation workers.

Dr. Martin Luther King, Jr., is buried in South View Cemetery in Atlanta.

FREE AT LAST, FREE AT LAST
THANK GOD ALMIGHTY
I'M FREE AT LAST

—Inscription on Martin Luther King's tomb

~ 1986 ~

On November 2, a national holiday is proclaimed in King's honor.

MARTIN LUTHER KING, JR. DAY
By the President of the United States of America
A PROCLAMATION

This year marks the first observance of the birthday of Dr. Martin Luther King, Jr. as a national holiday. It is a time for rejoicing and reflecting. We rejoice because, in his short life, Dr. King, by his preaching, by his example, and his leadership, helped to move us closer to the ideals on which America was founded. We reflect on his words and his works.

Dr. King's was truly a prophetic voice that reached out over the chasms of hostility, prejudice, ignorance, and fear to touch the conscience of America. He challenged us to make real the promise of America as a land of freedom, equality, opportunity, and brotherhood.

Although Dr. King was an uncompromising champion of nonviolence, he was often the victim of violence. And, as we know, a shameful act of violence cut short his life before he had reached his fortieth birthday.

His story is well-known. As a 26-year-old minister of the Gospel, Dr. King led a protest boycott of a bus company that segregated blacks, treating them as second-class citizens. At the very outset he admonished all those who would join in the protest that "our actions must be guided by the deepest principles of our Christian faith. Love must be our regulating ideal." Otherwise, he warned, "our protest will end up as a meaningless drama on the stage of history ... shrouded with ugly garments of shame." Dr. King's unshakable faith inspired others to resist the temptation to hate and fear. His protest became a triumph of courage and love.

Almost 30 years ago, on January 30, 1956, Dr. King stood amid the broken glass and splinters of his bombed-out front porch and calmed an angry crowd clamoring for vengeance. "We cannot solve this problem through retaliatory violence," he told them. Dr. King steadfastly opposed both the timid and those who counselled violence. To the former, he preached that "true peace is not merely the absence of tension; it is the presence of justice." To the latter, he said that "in the process of gaining our rightful place we must not be guilty of wrongful deeds."

Dr. King's activism was rooted in the true patriotism that cherishes America's ideals and strives to narrow the gap between those ideals and reality. He took his stand, he once explained, "because of my love for America and the sublime principles of liberty and equality on which she is founded." He wanted "to transform the jangling discords of our Nation into a beautiful symphony of brotherhood."

The majesty of his message, the dignity of his bearing, and the righteousness of his cause are a lasting legacy. In a few short years he changed America for all time. He made it possible for our nation to move closer to the ideals set forth in our Declaration of Independence: that all people are created equal and are endowed with inalienable rights that government has the duty to respect and protect.

Twenty-three years ago, Dr. King spoke to a quarter of a million Americans gathered near the Lincoln Memorial in Washington—and to tens of millions more watching on television. There he held up his dream for America like a bright banner:

"I have a dream," he said, "that my four little children will one day live in a Nation where they will not be judged by the color of their skin, but by the content of their character ... This will be the day when all of God's children will be able to sing with new meaning, 'My country 'tis of thee, sweet land of liberty, of thee I sing.' "

Let all Americans continue to carry forward the banner that 18 years ago fell from Dr. King's hands. Today, all over America, libraries, hospitals, parks, and thoroughfares proudly bear his name. His likeness appears on more than 100 postage stamps issued by dozens of nations around the globe. Today we honor him with speeches and monuments. But let us do more. Let all Americans of every race and creed and color work together to build in this blessed land a shining city of brotherhood, justice, and harmony. This is the monument Dr. King would have wanted most of all.

By Public Law 98–144, the third Monday in January of each year has been designated as a public holiday in honor of the "Birthday of Martin Luther King, Jr."

Now, therefore, I, Ronald Reagan, President of the United States of America, do hereby proclaim Monday, January 20, 1986, as Martin Luther King, Jr. Day. In witness whereof, I have hereunto set my hand this eighteenth day of January, in the year of our Lord nineteen hundred and eighty-six, and of the Independence of the United States of America the two hundred and tenth.

(signed) Ronald Reagan

NOTES TO
BIOGRAPHY

1934. "He told me . . ." (Garrow, *Bearing the Cross*, p. 33);
"Every parent . . ." (*Stride Toward Freedom*, p. 19); "My
mother . . ." (*Stride Toward Freedom*, p. 19).

1935–1940. "I remember a trip . . ." (*Stride Toward Freedom*, pp. 20–21).

1943–46. "During my early teens . . ." (*The Strength to
Love*, p. 137); "During my late teens . . ." (*Stride Toward
Freedom*, p. 90); "When I went to Atlanta's Morehouse . . ."
(*Stride Toward Freedom*, p. 91); "I had felt the urge . . ."
("An Autobiography of Religious Development," ca. 1949);
"I gained my major influences . . ." (*Crusader*, April 1957,
p. 7); "Not until I entered Crozer . . ." (*Stride Toward Free-
dom*, p. 91); "I was well aware . . ." (interview with Law-
rence Reddick, 1959); "One Sunday afternoon . . ." (*Stride
Toward Freedom*, p. 96).

1951–53. "I studied philosophy . . ." (*Stride Toward Freedom*, p. 100); "August of 1953 . . ." (*Stride Toward Freedom*,
p. 16).

1954. "I was very conscious . . ." (*Stride Toward Freedom*,
p. 17); "The question of my wife's . . ." (*Stride Toward Freedom*, p. 21).

1955. "As I thought further I came to see ..." (*Stride Toward Freedom*, p. 51); "As soon as Bennet ..." (*Stride Toward Freedom*, p. 57); "She did not need ..." (*Stride Toward Freedom*, p. 59); "We are here this evening ..." (speech, Dec. 5, 1955); "As I sat listening ..." (*Stride Toward Freedom*, p. 63); "And then we started ..." (Garrow, *Bearing the Cross*, p. 58); "And it seemed at that moment ..." (Garrow, *Bearing the Cross*, p. 58); "[1] We have discovered ..." (speech, Dec. 3, 1956).

1958. "I sat in a Harlem ..." (*Why We Can't Wait*, p. 17).

1959. "I left India ..." (*Hindustani Times*, March 9, 1959); "For almost four years ..." (sermon, Nov. 29, 1959).

1961. "The new administration ..." ("The President Has the Power," *Nation*, Feb. 4, 1961, p. 91).

1963. "As we neared ..." (*Why We Can't Wait*, p. 74); "Apparently the President ..." (*Why We Can't Wait*, p. 75); "I am in Birmingham ..." (Letter from Birmingham Jail, 1963); "The acceptance of responsibility ..." (statement, May 10, 1963); "In its entire glittering ..." (*Why We Can't Wait*, p. 123); "The March was the first ..." (*Why We Can't Wait*, p. 124); "I started out reading ..." (*interview, in* Garrow, p. 283).

1966. "I went home that night ..." (*Where Do We Go from Here?* p. 45); "For years I labored ..." (quoted in *Harper's*, August 1967, p. 48).

1967. "In 1963, on a sweltering ..." (*The Trumpet of Conscience*, p. 75); "We will place ..." (quoted in *Look*, April 15, 1969); "I left Atlanta ..." (speech, Memphis, April 3, 1968).

BIBLIOGRAPHY

Abernathy, Ralph. *And the Walls Came Tumbling Down.* Harper & Row, 1989.

Ansbro, John. *Martin Luther King, Jr.: The Making of a Mind.* Orbis Books, 1982.

Bennett, Lerone, Jr. *What Manner of Man.* Johnson Publishing Co., 1968.

Bornet, Vaughn Davis. *The Presidency of Lyndon B. Johnson.* University Press of Kansas, 1983.

Branch, Taylor. *Parting the Waters: America in the King Years, 1954–63.* Simon & Schuster, 1988.

Du Bois, W.E.B. *The Souls of Black Folk* (1903). Signet, 1969.

Garrow, David. *The FBI and Martin Luther King, Jr.* W.W. Norton, 1981.

Garrow, David. *Bearing the Cross: Martin Luther King, Jr., and the Southern Christian Leadership Conference.* William Morrow & Co., 1986.

Goodwin, Richard N. *Remembering America: A Voice from the Sixties.* Little, Brown & Co., 1988.

Grant, Joanne. *Black Protest: History, Documents, and Analysis, 1619 to Present.* Fawcett Premier, 1968.

Guthman, Edwin. *We Band of Brothers.* Harper & Row, 1971.

Halberstam, David. *The Best and the Brightest*. Random House, 1969.

Hampton, Henry and Steve Fayer, with Sarah Flynn. *Voices of Freedom: An Oral History of the Civil Rights Movement*. Bantam Books, 1990.

Haskins, James. *The Life and Death of Martin Luther King, Jr.* Lothrop, Lee & Shepard, 1977.

Haskins, James. *Andrew Young: Man with a Mission*. Lothrop, Lee & Shepard, 1979.

Johnson, Lyndon Baines. *The Vantage Point: Perspectives of the Presidency, 1963–1969*. Holt, Rinehart, and Winston, 1971.

Kaiser, Charles. *1968 in America: Music, Politics, Chaos, Counterculture, and the Shaping of a Generation*. Weidenfeld & Nicholson, 1988.

King, Coretta Scott. *My Life with Martin Luther King, Jr.* Holt, Rinehart, and Winston, 1969.

King, Coretta Scott. *The Words of Martin Luther King, Jr.* (Selected by Coretta Scott King). Newmarket Press, 1983.

King, Martin Luther, Jr. *Stride Toward Freedom: The Montgomery Story*. Harper & Brothers, 1958.

King, Martin Luther, Jr. *The Strength to Love*. Harper & Row, 1963.

King, Martin Luther, Jr. *Why We Can't Wait*. Harper & Row, 1963, 1964.

King, Martin Luther, Jr. *Where Do We Go from Here: Chaos or Community?* Harper & Row, 1967.

King, Martin Luther, Jr. *The Trumpet of Conscience*. Harper & Row, 1967.

King, Martin Luther, Sr., with Clayton Riley. *Daddy King: An Autobiography*. William Morrow, 1980.

Lewis, David L. *King: A Biography*. University of Illinois Press, 1970, 1978.

Mays, Benjamin. *Born to Rebel*. Charles Scribner's Sons, 1971.

Oates, Stephen B. *Let the Trumpet Sound: The Life of Martin Luther King, Jr.* New American Library, 1982.

Patterson, Lillie. *Martin Luther King, Jr. and the Freedom Movement*. Facts on File, 1989.

Playboy Interviews (selected by the editors of *Playboy*), Playboy Press, 1967.

Reddick, Lawrence D. *Crusader Without Violence: A Biography of Martin Luther King, Jr*. Harper & Brothers, 1959.

Rustin, Bayard. *Down the Line: The Collected Writings of Bayard Rustin*. Quadrangle, 1971.

Schlesinger, Arthur M., Jr. *A Thousand Days: John F. Kennedy in the White House*. Houghton Mifflin, 1965.

Schlesinger, Arthur M., Jr. *Robert Kennedy and His Times*. Houghton Mifflin, 1978.

Schulke, Flip, and Penelope O. McPhee. *King Remembered*. W.W. Norton, 1986.

Smith, K. L., and Ira G. Zepp. *The Search for the Beloved Community: The Thinking of Martin Luther King*. Judson Press, 1974.

Stein, Jean, with George Plimpton. *American Journey: The Times of Robert Kennedy*. Harcourt Brace Jovanovich, 1970.

Sullivan, William, with Bill Brown. *The Bureau: My Thirty Years In Hoover's FBI*. W.W. Norton, 1979.

U.S. House of Representatives. *The Final Assassinations Report: Report of the Select Committee on Assassinations*. Bantam, 1979.

U.S. Senate. Report No. 94–755. Supplementary Detailed Staff Reports on Intelligence Activities and the Rights of Americans. *Book III: Final Report*. U.S. Government Printing Office, 1976.

Walker, Wyatt Tee. *Somebody's Calling My Name: Black Sacred Music and Social Change*. Judson Press, 1979.

White, Theodore H. *The Making of the President 1964*. Atheneum Publishers, 1965.

Williams, John A. *The King God Didn't Save*. Coward, 1970.

Wofford, Harris. *Of Kennedys and Kings: Making Sense of the Sixties*. Farrar, Straus, Giroux, 1980.